# Os Guinness
# The Gravedigger File

## Papers on the Subversion of the Modern Church

Cover illustration
by Guy Wolek

Cartoons by
Nick Butterworth

*INTER-VARSITY PRESS*
*DOWNERS GROVE*
*ILLINOIS 60515*

InterVarsity Press is the book-publishing division of Inter-Varsity Christian Fellowship, a student movement active on campus at hundreds of universities, colleges and schools of nursing. For information about local and regional activities, write IVCF, 233 Langdon St., Madison, WI 53703.

Distributed in Canada through InterVarsity Press, 860 Denison St., Unit 3, Markham, Ontario L3R 4H1, Canada.

ISBN 0-87784-817-3

Printed in the United States of America

**Library of Congress Cataloging in Publication Data**
Guinness, Os.
    The gravedigger file.

    Includes bibliographical references.
    1. Christianity–20th century.    2. Secularization
(Theology)    I. Title.
BR481.G84    1983            270.8'2            83-10666
ISBN 0-87784-817-3

| 17 | 16 | 15 | 14 | 13 | 12 | 11 | 10 | 9 | 8 | 7 | 6 | 5 | 4 | 3 | 2 | 1 |
| 95 | 94 | 93 | 92 | 91 | 90 | 89 | 88 | 87 | 86 | 85 | 84 | 83 | | | | |

D.O.M
and to
David and Suzy Young,
dear friends
and unquestionably among the exceptions

# Grateful Acknowledgments

To Professor Peter L. Berger, Professor David Martin, Professor Basil Mitchell, Mr. Malcolm Muggeridge and Dr. Bryan Wilson—for the inspiration and challenge of their thinking, writing and teaching, and for the unfailing helpfulness of their counsel.

To Gini Andrews, David Cook, Joan Lloyd Guest, Roger Henderson, George and Victoria Hobson, Doug and Ann Holladay, David Lyon, Graeme McLean, David Prior, Franky Schaeffer, James Sire, Carsten Thiede, Michael and Jean Woodruff, David and Suzy Young, my mother and father, members of the Carmen Deo Community in Santa Barbara and the staff of Bel Air Presbyterian Church—for their invaluable criticism of this book, and for their friendship and stimulation which have been the matrix in which these ideas have been developed.

To June Berk, Sharon Candell, Betty Ho Sang, Kathy Paver and Elaine Schmidt—for their tireless willingness and skill in deciphering and typing an almost illegible scribble.

To Jenny—whose name should really be on the cover of this book. My dearest friend and toughest critic.

## Foreword:
## How These Papers Came into My Hands

My wife and I have known the source of these papers for five or six years, first in the setting of his graduate philosophy seminars, then in the wider context of university life and, more recently, as an occasional dinner guest in our own home. To all appearances, he was a typical university don, genial, witty and (when occasion served) penetrating in his insights and criticism. Not once in all these years has he ever given us a clue that this was a mask for an altogether different self.

We had sometimes talked quite deeply, though always agreeing to differ over the question of our respective convictions. Trained, as I realize now, to withstand forms of interrogation somewhat stronger than philosophy seminars, he must have listened to us and nonchalantly parried the questions we raised like an adult playing chess with children.

The break came when we were dining together at his college, after an invitation which was uncharacteristically late and insistent. I noticed that he seemed distracted, almost agitated. He chose to sit at the end of the table, well out of the central conversation. Once the main course had been served and the conversation level was rising around the dining hall, he dropped his voice, a sudden edge entering it.

"Look," he said, "I need your help. Listen to me carefully, but show no sign of any special attention. It's possible that I'm being watched. I suggested meeting here because it was less conspicuous than coming to your home."

"I believe I can trust you," he continued. "I've come to see where your North Star lies. And there's one other person I know I can trust... Old Fool indeed!"

The last three words were said more to himself than to me; they trailed off into the unlit world of his own thoughts. In response to my questioning look, he spoke the name of a distinguished writer whom he knew I had recently interviewed.

"I will soon need to get something to him urgently, without fail. I gather you've met him. Are you willing to do it?" If so, he continued, he would contact me again in the course of the next week. He was waiting for the arrival of something which would allow him to act.

His call came earlier than I expected. At home the next evening the phone was ringing as I let myself in. He wanted me to meet him that night. "Radcliffe Square. Catte Street entrance, 11 P.M.," he said and rang off without further explanation.

The deep bell of the University Church was tolling over the almost deserted square as he loomed out of the misty November night under the winter flowering cherry tree. Under his arm was a white paper bag with the familiar *Blackwell's* trademark. He thrust it into my hands and, seizing my arm, piloted me brusquely across the square and on toward Broad Street.

We walked together for only fifteen minutes before he slipped into the darkness as silently as he had arrived. In the bag, he said, I would find some top secret memos directed to him, which I should take the next morning to the writer he had mentioned. Together we should get them published without delay. He was emphatic about the urgency. He would be missed as soon as he failed to turn up for a flight at Heathrow, so twelve hours were all that were left him. The writer wouldn't be expecting the papers, but would know what to do. He had also been a journalist and had worked in intelligence, so he would appreciate immediately what sort of thing he was dealing with.

"With the proviso that you add an afterword of your own," he said, "you can publish them just as they stand. For six years you've been arguing the case for the Christian faith and saying there was another side to the church; that my facts weren't all the facts. Now you must write about it to put these papers in perspective. But the papers must be published at once. It's urgent that Christians should realize what's happening." And then he added cryptically, "We'll see whether the Director is right."

He told me many things besides this, things which have been weighing on my mind ever since, some of which I will discuss in the afterword. Finally, he said he would be leaving Oxford that night to go into hiding on the Continent; from there he would contact me after the public response to the papers was clear. He would be very interested to see the official response, but that wasn't his ultimate concern; it was the popular response that would prove decisive.

Also in the bag were some cartoons which were his own doodled accompaniment to the papers. These have been published too, for in a sense the seeds of his defection were nurtured by the comic perspective which lay behind them. There were no footnotes in the original papers. The references have been traced wherever possible and added to the text for those wishing to delve more deeply into the thinking behind the papers.

I have followed his instructions to the letter and with the cooperation of the writer am now presenting these papers to a wider audience so that, just as our source urgently requested, the papers can speak for themselves.

The last thing he said to me was this: "Maybe even the Doomsday clock has more time than the Western church."

*Os Guinness*
*Oxford*

# MEMORANDUM
## 1

**SUBJECT:**
# OPERATION GRAVEDIGGER
**FROM:**
DEPUTY DIRECTOR,
CENTRAL SECURITY COUNCIL
**TO:**
DIRECTOR DESIGNATE,
LOS ANGELES BUREAU
**CLASSIFICATION:**
ULTRA SECRET

■

Warmest congratulations, both on your appointment as head of the Los Angeles Bureau and on your election to the Central Security Council. I have followed your steady rise in the service for some time. I have also consistently argued that Los Angeles deserves permanent representation on the Council. As you are well aware, not everyone takes this position. But we are confident that you will soon convince those who have reservations about you personally as well as those who fail to see the strategic importance of upgrading the L.A. Bureau. I say *we* advisedly. With the Director favoring it, your election was a formality and went through on the nod.

Naturally, it will be a wrench for you to leave Oxford. The mist and rain you may not miss. But what other place rivals its intellectual sophistication, its urbanity and wit, all wreathed in the smoke of endless pipes and washed down with sherry and port? You will soon discover that Los Angeles has its own compensations. But my excitement for you goes beyond a question of place. Moving from Oxford to L.A. is more than a change of cities. It will mean a switch in strategies that you will find engrossing.

You are taking over in Los Angeles just when it is becoming crucial to our plans. Many people think Hollywood's greatest days are over. They miss the point. Our sights are on the wider influence of the Beverly Hills community, especially as it takes the lead in the media revolution. Link that to the microchip revolution and the power of Silicon Valley further north; L.A. will be the software capital of the media world and one of the bellwether cities of the future. Talk of the "Los Angelization" of the world is a little far-fetched, but the California connection will undoubtedly become one of our hottest lines of activity.

The Director himself has asked me to brief you on our top priority operation. You have three more months in England before you take up your new post. This will allow you to give the Operation your undivided attention, as well as to fit in some advance trips to L.A. It will take some work catching up on the background, which I'll be sending you. Master the details, but don't lose sight of the wood for the trees. The big picture is what counts.

**Operation Gravedigger**
We are poised on the brink of a staggering victory. Reports from all fronts of the modernized sector of the world indicate that, after two hundred fifty years of painstaking planning and successful preliminary operations, the payoff is very close. Operation Gravedigger is moving smoothly and inexorably toward its climax. Its goal— the complete neutralization of the modern Western church by subversion from within—is in sight and almost in our grasp.

I will be sending you memos from week to week to brief you on the Operation and the part your Bureau is to play. In this first memo, I will define the Operation, its objectives and assumptions.

I will also outline aspects of the Operation which will be examined more fully in subsequent memoranda.

The underlying strategy of Operation Gravedigger is as stark in its simplicity as it is devastating in its results. It may be stated like this: *Christianity contributed to the rise of the modern world; the modern world, in turn, has undermined Christianity; Christianity has become its own gravedigger.*[1] The strategy turns on this monumental irony, and the victory we are so close to realizing depends on two elementary insights. First, that Christianity is now becoming captive to the very "modern world" it helped to create. Second, that our interests are best served, not by working *against* the church, but by working *with* it. The more the church becomes one with the modern world, the more it becomes compromised, and the deeper the grave it digs for itself.

Having come in on the Operation when it was already well advanced, my own contribution has been minimal; so my use of the word *we* in these memos is in the broad, organizational sense. But as you will come to recognize, the very relentlessness of the way the strategy is being carried out betrays its mastermind. Only one mind is capable of such audacity of vision and sheer force of will. "God is in the detail," people say. If only they knew.

*A fall beyond belief.* Now that the final phase of the Operation is beginning, a wider distribution of information is needed, and the Operation will soon be downgraded from "ultra secret" to "top secret." This is not to be taken as a sign of relaxing urgency. The art of "controlled leaks" has become a finely tuned instrument of state policy, but incidents such as the disclosure of the Pentagon Papers show how leak-prone classified information still is. Indeed, governments have long lamented that the ship of state is the only vessel that leaks from the top and not the bottom. Now, with the invention of the photocopier, the vessel is holed irreparably.

Our own record over security leaks is unrivaled and will remain so. But there are several on the Council who query whether the enemy still has the capacity to profit from any disclosure of the Operation. There is no question of our risking the strategy by putting this belief to the test, but at the same time the reasons for such a belief are compelling.

There is, first, a psychological reason. Even if the details were leaked, the enemy's most likely reaction would be disbelief. I will explain later why we are able to count on such a response, but it allows us to press forward, rather as Hitler was able to discount possible Allied reaction to news about Auschwitz: "But they will never believe it." You can take this complacency (or its opposite extreme, the credulity that believes in any and every conspiracy) as a measure of our success so far.

In any case, they would never take the trouble to make sense of these papers. Most Christians, as a current jibe runs, would rather die than think—in fact they do. If sections of their handbook such as the letter to the Romans had been addressed to a modern church, they would doubtless be rejected as too complicated, too intellectual.

The Director was the first to maintain that even if this material were leaked, it would cause little stir. I have learned to bow to his judgment. With sales up and serious thought down, Christian publishing and reading are approaching the point where inspiring deep reflection and reformation will be beyond the Bible itself. The conspiracy-prone fringe and the complacent majority are as bad as each other. The former cannot see clearly because they only see red; the latter do not read seriously, so they cannot see at all.

There is also a strategic reason for our confidence. The Operation is moving into a phase which is almost irreversible. History tends to mock the finality of judgments such as irresistible or irreversible, yet such claims are not far off. Your role in Operation Gravedigger is not to be a theoretician, let alone historian, so I will spare you a lengthy historical overview. However, to give yourself some simple historical back-bearings, it's useful to chart the development of the Operation against the course of the First and Second Industrial Revolutions.

*The darkest hour just before dawn.* When the First Industrial Revolution began in the mid-eighteenth century, we were caught unawares, and the situation appeared to be getting out of control. Massive spiritual awakening was sweeping Britain and the American colonies under the leadership of John Wesley and George White-field (both Oxford men, incidentally—a lamentable stain on the record of your former Bureau).

This period of spiritual awakening coincided with rapid social and technological change. The "power of the Spirit" and the power of steam made a devastating partnership. The danger they created was that Christianity would become the leading contributor to what the rest of the world would see and experience as the leading societies in the newly industrializing world.

This threat was partly fulfilled in early nineteenth-century England. The evangelical faith of the heirs of Wesley and Whitefield grew so strong that it was actually described as "the single, most widespread influence in Victorian England"[2] and "the rock on which the character of the nineteenth century English was founded."[3]

That dark hour in the mid-eighteenth century was our Dunkirk, and it led to what is known in the trade as a duck dive. But it also forced the Council into the rethinking from which Operation Gravedigger was launched. We could not forestall such a momentous convergence of spiritual revival and social revolution. At least, not in the English-speaking world. But if our counter-offensive succeeded, we could channel that power so that it would eventually become self-subverting.

Now, more than two centuries later, we are well into the Second Industrial Revolution. The development of computers and the microchip have shifted the emphasis from a technology of muscle to one of mind; and the lead society is no longer Britain but the United States. This is the decisive stage in the course of Operation Gravedigger. Curiously, the evangelicals are now bidding to come to center stage in the U.S. just as they did in England a hundred fifty years ago, but with even less chance of success, as will become clear. By the end of the 1980s, the "mighty micro" will have made its own irrevocable impact on the modern world. When the effect of this compounds the forces of modernization unleashed over the

past two hundred years, the success of Operation Gravedigger will be assured.

This prediction may strike you as sweeping and overconfident. But once I have outlined the entire operation, you will appreciate the concrete base on which it rests. You may be doubtful that so complete a collapse can be achieved in so short a time. This reaction would come from a weakness in the "intellectualist" tradition in which you've been trained. I will pick that up later.

For the moment, simply savor the breathtaking prospect of the church in checkmate. Our ancient knights and rooks are pressing deep into the defense that surrounds the Christian king. The Director has withdrawn into himself with a concentration and a stillness that can be felt. The present stage of the Operation is charged with high-voltage tension like the moment between lightning and thunder.

### Operational Assumptions

Although Operation Gravedigger is essentially simple and its impact obvious, its underlying assumptions are quite subtle. In planning the Operation, we found two principles especially important.

*1. The way of the fox, rather than the lion.*   When Louis XIV went out to battle, he had inscribed on his cannons: *Ultima ratio regum* ("the final argument of kings"). There in a nutshell is the philosophy of the big stick and the big battalions. Unfortunately for the Sun King, the Duke of Marlborough carried an even bigger stick and commanded even stronger battalions.

We were not going to make such a mistake. We knew that open warfare could not succeed. It depends on the basic maxim, "If you don't win, you lose," and the late-eighteenth-century alliance of Spirit and steam had left us outnumbered and outgunned in the English-speaking world. The situation was different in France, of course—thanks to Voltaire and the Roman Catholic church —but our first concern was England. We could rely there on certain heavy artillery (such as the skepticism of David Hume from north of the border), but taking everything into account, all-out attach was not an attractive proposition.

The secret of clandestine warfare, by contrast, lies in the maxim, "If you don't lose, you win." Ever since Machiavelli, Western statesmen and politicians have been fascinated with the idea of combining the wiles of the fox with the strength of the lion. We have used both to effect, but this time we knew victory lay the way of the fox. If war (in Clausewitz's dictum) is the extension of politics by other means, clandestine war is the extension of conventional war by other means.

The task, therefore, was to engage the church in a relentless war without frontiers, becoming the invisible, melting enemy, creating the everywhere-and-nowhere feeling in a struggle that went far beyond the clash of arguments and swords. The arguments and the swords were there, but more as a cover behind which we could use subversion and infiltration to advance steadily, picking off vulnerable areas one by one. This was to be a struggle in many ways more difficult than open warfare, one in which victory was achieved person by person and piece by piece, without an argument ever heard to be won or a church ever seen to be repressed.

This strategy of subversion has followed certain overlapping stages, some of which we are completing only in the present generation. The first stage was *penetration* (or "worming in"), the step through which our agents have infiltrated Christian groups and organizations with a view to manipulating them.

The second stage was *demoralization* (or "softening up"), the stage at which we worked to ruin the fabric of the church's spiritual and social life so that morale sagged and Christians slowly became incapable of effective resistance. "The thing now"—as Marx put his version of the tactic—"is to instill poison wherever possible."[4] This is the same demoralizing tactic which the Nazis recently used with such skill (their word for it was *zersetsung*, or "tearing apart") that it went to their heads.

The third stage has been *subversion* (or "winning over"), the step through which we have worked to win the hearts and minds of key members of the church. Behind this move is the recognition that the church's morale and will to resist depend on its loyalty to the Adversary and to certain of his symbols such as his word or sacraments. These are the flag and emblems of the Christian nation, and it is loyalty to these which we have had to detach carefully and transfer.

We will never subvert all Christians, of course. All we need is a _passive acceptance_ by the general body of Christians on the one hand and a _positive allegiance_ by a carefully selected counter-elite on the other. Without this counter-elite we could never hope to win, let alone establish, our own rule.

The fourth stage has been _defection_ (or "bringing over" individual Christians), the stage through which we have kept up sustained propaganda designed to make the most of notorious defections from the Christian side (counter-conversions, if you like). The high tide for this sort of brain drain was the late-nineteenth century (hence the current shortage of serious Christian thinking). But don't overrate such defections. Like that of defectors and émigrés in today's Cold War, the value of counter-conversions and anti-testimonies diminishes with time. Today the shock headline, tomorrow the old bore and the chronic refugee.

The final stage, which still lies ahead, is _liberation_ (or the "taking over" of the whole church). This is the stage at which the degree of our influence will become absolute, and the secret operation will become public—through _coup d'état_. That, obviously, is our supreme objective and the one we are actually approaching in this momentous generation.

All this can be distilled into what the Director calls "10-10-80," a key concept you will need to apply repeatedly. How many times I have watched him listen to devastating reports in cold silence and then utter the words: "Remember 10-10-80." It is simply the shorthand for his own axiom: Win over ten per cent of the church to be a counter-elite on our side, reduce eighty per cent of the church to a state of passive acceptance (either cowed or complacent), and we can disregard the active resistance of the remaining ten per cent (part of which is the lunatic fringe anyway).

This latter ten percent is a particularly important category. It allows us a margin of error. It also takes into account all those exceptions to the trends we are manipulating successfully. If such exceptions were ever to amount to more than ten per cent, we would have to bring in the contingency plans. But for a long time we have been well within this limit.

**2. *Subvert strength, rather than attack weakness.*** This second principle takes the first even further and has proved quite decisive. Indeed, it lies at the heart of the entire Operation. The church's most crucial weakness is found at the point of her most conspicuous strength.

The tactic is as old as time. A person's or group's strong point often becomes an unguarded point. This, as any English schoolboy knows, is amply illustrated in military disasters from the fall of Croesus' "impregnable" Sardis in 549 B.C. to the fall of Singapore in 1942. (The British Empire's mightiest naval base fell ignominiously to "little men on bicycles" who easily stormed the notorious fifteen-inch guns which were facing the wrong way.)[5] Each was unguarded at its strongest point. But there is something less obvious and more important to us. A person's true strengths are not only likely to be left exposed; they can easily be turned inside out and made into real weaknesses.

Inversion, or turning things inside out and upside-down, is, of course, the heart of the revolution we are out to promote. The relative is made to bear the weight of the absolute, and finite people and things are given the place of the infinite (the "creature rather than the Creator," as their handbook puts it).[6]

What happens when one strand of reality is singled out and stretched too far is hardly surprising. Wider reality springs back and has the last laugh. Pressed too far, for example, reason becomes rationalism and rebounds into mysticism; or freedom becomes anarchy and rebounds into authoritarianism. We thus become masters of irony, connoisseurs of the art of the unintended consequence. Reality rebounds, and things turn out the opposite of what they seem and what people expect. Strength becomes weakness, love pornography, pleasure boredom and so on.

We have had classic successes with this tactic in the lives of individuals. We call it the Samson syndrome because you see the cycle so clearly in the namesake. Trace the line from his early promise, to his extraordinary exploits, to his careless delinquency and ultimate downfall. Samson could become prodigal only because his strength was prodigious. When his gifts became his master, they were the key to his undoing. Et voilà, strength turned to weakness. "All men that are ruined," said Edmund Burke, "are ruined on the side of their natural propensities."[7]

We have sometimes pulled this off with whole nations, but it usually takes longer, and in the mid-eighteenth century time was what we lacked. What if, through an authentic spiritual revival, Christianity were to gain a decisive influence in Britain and America at the very time when those nations (through modernization) were gaining a decisive influence in the world? In one leap the Enemy would have been around the world, and centuries of work would have been undone. There was no time to lose. We had to put out the fire of Western revival where it started before its sparks could be carried to some dry corner of the world less easily dealt with.

Our long-term objective was clear: to work out the best way to turn the church's strengths into weaknesses and turn their enormous advantage into a disadvantage. Once we found this, we could parody their own approach ("perverting" rather than "perfecting" their strength in weakness) and use it to plan our boldest operation.

This is how the Council's thinking developed. To begin, the researchers and archivists were set to work on a full-scale re-examination and analysis of Christian beliefs and behavioral requirements. Despite the accepted wisdom that the ideal attack-point was faith, we insisted on starting from scratch and hunting for any new lines of inquiry which might have provided us with background on the problem at hand. Might there be some key flaw or potential stress-point we had overlooked in earlier studies?

The "burrowers" were magnificent. No lines of inquiry were overlooked. Personal files, subject files, method files, background files. They rechecked every last one. Never have they worked over anything with such thoroughness, but their findings were always the same. The crucial point of strain for Christians is ultimately their faith.

The job then was to crack the secret of the workings of faith. Or as it's put in the trade, to analyze their handwriting—trade jargon for their habits and patterns of behavior. As you know, the philosophical strength of Christianity lies in its *claim to truth,* whereas the social strength of Christianity lies in its *challenge to tension.* It was at this second point that the break came. Let me explain.

Part of the root meaning of the word *faith* is "tension" or "tautness." There in two words is an accurate picture of the faith required of Christians. And there's the rub. Loyalty to the Adversary in a world liberated by us makes their lives a kind of "double wrestling."[8] Faithfulness to him has to mean foreignness in the world. As they put it themselves, they are to live in a way that is clearly distinct in terms of space ("in" the world but not "of" it) and in terms of time ("no longer" what they were, "not yet" what they will be). Their unenviable role, as one of them has it, is to be *"against* the world *for* the world."[9] Let them try telling that to their next-door neighbors.

Such a high-wire balancing act would be precarious at best, even if the poise it entails were all that's required of them. But that is not the case, and here a further element is introduced. The Adversary has actually *commanded* them to be identified with the world. From his perspective, there are still a great number of positive reasons for their being in the world, the most basic of which is to seek to reclaim it for him.

Here is where we saw their ancient Achilles' heel at its most exposed. If any of these "positive" purposes of cultural involvement could be overdeveloped, they would serve to obscure the growing negative side effects. For instance, if their desire to witness leads to cultural involvement, cultural involvement leads in turn to the danger of worldliness. The price of contact would be contamination.

This cultural contamination could happen in any culture. How much easier, though, would it be to achieve in a culture which Christians regard as good because they themselves had contributed to its creation?

What the Council envisaged has worked out exactly. From the initial research to the present moment, no operation has ever gone better, and Gravedigger is sure to become a classic in subversion through culture. The textbook procedure has been followed with such ease that you, with your philosophical training as a counter-apologist, would find it absurd. The church contributed to the creation of the modern world. Soon she was committed to that world without reservation. Before long she was hopelessly contaminated—in the world and up to her neck.

We have moved easily through the standard levels of subversion, each level leaving the church deeper in cultural captivity. First, we encouraged the complete identification of the church with culture so that she couldn't see where one ended and the other began. This is the *culture-blind* level, the level at which we have neutralized her integrity.

Second, we developed this identification of church and culture to the point where she had no strength to act independently. This is the *culture-bound* level, the level at which we have neutralized her effectiveness either to do anything distinctively different from the culture or to be seen as different by others.

Now we are approaching the *culture-burnt* level. This is the level at which it becomes apparent (too late) that, through her uncritical identification with culture, the church has been badly burned and must live with the consequences. Our supreme prize at this level is the complete devastation of the church by getting the Adversary to judge her himself.

Here you see the heart of the Council's design. To this point the focus has been on the church's being subverted as her cultural strengths are turned into weaknesses. But now, enter the Adversary. When we manage to see that his gifts, such as the fruits of culture, are subtly changed and become idols, he changes too—from giver to judge. In fact, some of his most severe judgments have been against *his own gifts and works once they are idolized.*

The clearest precedents for this are found in his own records. It is most revealing to follow them through. Who killed a man for daring to touch the ark of his covenant, but carelessly let it fall into enemy hands when it was treated as a talisman? Who was most against the Temple in Jerusalem (which he himself designed) once it was abused? Who attacked the rules surrounding the Sabbath that he himself had ordained? Or the Law which he himself had laid down? Who keeps reiterating the theme of destroying what he himself has built, uprooting what he has planted? When his own gifts and works are misused, no one is more against them than the Adversary.[10]

There lay the guarantee of our success. Under certain circumstances, the Adversary could be counted on to act as a sort of *agent extraordinaire* and do our work for us. All that remained was to find the most suitable gifts against which he would be forced to move once they were perverted. *His own transcendence would then become subversive. There is nothing, short of himself, which he might not have to judge and destroy.*

Here in a stroke is the beauty of subversion through worldliness and its infinite superiority to persecution. Persecution is the world's drastic action to deal with the foreign body in its midst; judgment is the Adversary's drastic action to deal with the foreignness in the midst of his body. If the Adversary is to judge his own people, who are we to complain?

**Operation Outline**
I only have time now to outline the Operation, but I intend to take up details in later memoranda. This briefing can be divided into three main parts. Part one covers the *conception of the project.* I have just dealt with this briefly here, but will elaborate in a second memo. Part two analyzes the rise of the modern world and the overwhelming pressures it brings to bear on the Christian faith. The three key pressures to be discussed are *secularization,* or the Cheshire-cat factor; *privatization,* or the private-zoo factor; and *pluralization,* or the smorgasbord factor. This second section will deal with *concentrating pressures* on the church.

Part three will analyze what contamination by culture has meant for: first, Christian institutions; second, Christian ideas; and third, Christian involvement in the world. This section will deal with *creating problems* for the church.

The stage we have reached is critical. The Christian faith has been challenged by new environments before, but never has it faced as massive a threat as it faces from modernization now. No age, no culture, no civilization has ever represented such unmeasurable and unmanageable realities or carried such an unparalleled capacity to shape the lives of its members. In the spirit of modernity, the spirit of faith does not know what it is up against. It has finally met its match.

The modern world has risen up through and reached beyond Christianity, and now it is essentially no longer Christian. Such progress can never be reversed; such autonomy can never be recalled. The father has produced a son; and now the son has come of age and is locked in mortal combat with the father.

With the dawn of the microchip revolution, the countdown of our operation has begun. You could hardly have been more fortunate in the timing of your promotion. Again, my congratulations. The prospect of working with you gives me great pleasure.

# MEMORANDUM
## 2

**SUBJECT:**
## THE SANDMAN
## EFFECT
**FROM:**
DEPUTY DIRECTOR,
CENTRAL SECURITY COUNCIL
**TO:**
DIRECTOR DESIGNATE,
LOS ANGELES BUREAU
**CLASSIFICATION:**
ULTRA SECRET

■

Your response to my memo was exactly what I'd hoped. I anticipated the intense interest with which you responded to Operation Gravedigger, as well as your questions. Not for nothing does your dossier include the comment: "Loves philosophic jousting." I also wanted to see how you would take my needling over your intellectualism.

Some agents never succeed in adapting from counter-apologetics to cultural subversion, and a major reason is their snobbery. Once trained in the sophisticated methods of intellectual subversion, they consider other approaches beneath them and miss the chance to use simpler but equally effective strategies. European skepticism is a deadly weapon, but its use is limited. Being groomed for the highest posts, as you are, you would do well to add to it a complete mastery of the approach I'm outlining.

## A Surprising Discovery

Let me pick up the story again and elaborate on a key contribution to our success so far—the church's extraordinary vulnerability to our approach. This is also the best reply to the questions you raised about the strategy. Your point is well taken that irony isn't the exclusive property of either side, and that Philistines throwing parties should beware of Samsons who lean on pillars. Who had the last laugh is therefore a moot point, but one that is not at stake here. As you will see, our Samson is asleep.

In the beginning of the project, when the Council had agreed on the main objectives and strategy of the Operation, they sent an outline of the plans to various central departments for preliminary testing and development. The Department of Intelligence and the Department of Propaganda and Disinformation were the top priority, since their respective roles in the Operation were recognized as primary.

The response was rather remarkable. The traditional independence, if not rivalry, of these two departments is well known and has long provided us at the CSC with an extra source of criticism for all our planning. But in this case their reports revealed an unusual, early degree of consensus.

Each had arrived independently at the same conclusion. The plan to subvert the church by infiltrating it through culture was not only a striking *strategic opportunity* as we had expected; it also exposed the surprising *defensive vulnerability* of the church. All our data and experience since then have confirmed the accuracy of those early reports. We had stumbled on a front where the church was asleep and nearly defenseless. Hence "the sandman effect," the way in which contemporary Christians have a habit of falling asleep, even in the face of extreme danger.

You will have read regular intelligence reports on the increasingly derelict state of the Christian mind. In the early days the Council had checked similar reports to see whether the church was likely to respond critically and coherently if our proposed approach were discovered. (Of course, your former Bureau has played a magnificent part in creating the disarray which has existed since the Enlightenment. I needn't remind you of that.) It was then that they found what no one had anticipated. The church's defensive vulnerability was so complete that Christians were never likely even to detect our operation, let alone to respond. That is still the case.

Apparently, what finally convinced several of the Council to proceed with the Operation was the unusually low budget submitted by Propaganda and Disinformation. For once they had proposed no grandiose schemes and no padded expense accounts. Their plans were built on the recognition that, when the process of cultural subversion had gained momentum, little extra effort would be required. Ninety per cent of the resources needed to dig the church's grave would be her own.

Their original assessment of the church's vulnerability to cultural subversion was based on three crucial factors. Taken together, these produce the curious sandman effect. Instead of the church becoming more alert as cultural danger approaches, she falls into a deeper and deeper sleep. This makes it almost impossible for her to detect any subversion along cultural lines. I want to lay these factors out for you here, partly to demonstrate how the Operation has proceeded and partly to show you what this switch in strategies will mean for you personally. Remarkably enough, the three factors are even more relevant today than they were at the genesis of the Operation two hundred fifty years ago.

### No Feel for the Social Dimension of Believing

Most Christians have no trouble seeing themselves as "believers." They may be vague about what they believe and vaguer still about why they believe, but they believe. Fortunately, few have looked into the deeper dimensions of the nature of believing. After all, how can they be expected to understand the subtleties of belief in a world in which believing is hard enough? A dedicated minority have explored the intellectual dimensions of belief, and this is potentially dangerous to us. But even they have mostly tended to overlook the social dimensions. This oversight is our opportunity.

Let me describe something of my own experience to make clear what I mean by this first factor. It will also show that I appreciate how demanding the switch in strategies will be for you. You may know that before being appointed to the CSC I had worked for over twenty years on the Left Bank in Paris. What you wouldn't guess is that it was there, in that high-octane cerebral atmosphere, that I learned to go beyond subversion by purely intellectual means.

You can imagine my pleasure when, straight out of training, I was assigned not only to France but to Paris, and that tiny strip of Paris from which has flowed so much of its brilliance, creativity and skepticism. At first, the assignment was all I'd expected and more. The Bureau chief was a protégé of the Director. It was the early 1930s, and a dazzling array of "committed intellectuals" was assembling— Gide, Picasso, Malraux, Buñuel, Sartre, de Beauvoir, Ehrenburg and a score of lesser lights.

The combination of illustrious minds, formidable gifts, passionate debate and international influence was intoxicating. Every gesture and word from the Rive Gauche seemed to secure an immediate worldwide audience. I thought that there in that scintillating "republic of professors" was the potential for a worldwide movement of militant skepticism in the best tradition of earlier Left Bank heroes such as Voltaire.

I couldn't have been more naive. The Left Bank was to be a crucial influence, all right—for two and a half fascinating decades—but not at all in the way I'd expected. In spite of all the reputations and the promise, no great work of art was produced by those committed intellectuals during those years. Only loners, such as Camus, were exceptions. (The London equivalent of this—"Sohoitis"—was the contagious disease of talking books and art but never getting any work done.)[1] More extraordinarily still, our Bureau chief hardly bothered to encourage any major arguments against faith. He was after a different end.

The longer I served in Paris the more I understood and respected his strategy. In the first place, he was always as much interested in intellectual style as in the substance of intellectual debate. Long after the details of arguments were forgotten, he said, their aftertaste would linger, affecting the memory far more than the details ever had.

Think of the reputation of the Left Bank in the thirties and forties. Yes, there was brilliance, but its darker side was the empty rhetoric, the hypocritical poses, the shabby compromises, the betrayal of friends and causes, some people fellow-traveling with the Communists, others more or less sleeping with fascism.

As the chief anticipated, the legacy of this kind of general mood became a more effective innoculation against faith than a hundred Voltairean arguments. The desire for truth itself went out of fashion.

Also, and here again I came to see the influence of the Director, the chief was always more concerned with creating a whole world of skepticism than with merely producing a handful of skeptical individuals. This was the finesse of his strategy on the Left Bank. He knew that seen one way, the Left Bank was just a narrow strip of old houses and even older streets along the Seine where writers and artists lived and worked. But seen another way, it was a world of shared schools, such as the Sorbonne and the Ecole Normale Supérieure, shared literary salons, shared bookshops and publishing houses, and shared cafés, such as the Deux Magots, the Flore and Brasserie Lipp.

The effect? The Left Bank was not so much an address as an ambiance and an attitude of mind, not so much a place as a philosophy of life. "Revolution," as Clara Malraux observed, "is seeing each other a lot."[2]

Do you see how all this applies to you? Los Angeles (or London or Lagos for that matter) is important to us, not so much as a location as a mentality, a way of life, a world of its own. Yet that's exactly what the Christians overlook, because they have no feel for the social dimension of believing. Let me explain.

In a world unaffected by either our infiltration or our propaganda, the credibility of any belief would be determined simply by whether it were true or false. It would be believed if, and only if, it were objectively true; and if it were false, it would be quite literally incredible. I don't need to belabor the point.

Needless to say, such a state of affairs would eventually place us (to put no finer point on it) in rather an awkward light. But an excellent consequence of an earlier operation has been that this handicap has been lifted. It doesn't take a cynic to see that, since the truth requirement has been lifted, a climate has been created in which flagrant nonsense or complete error can be believed, and incontrovertible truth, in turn, can be disbelieved—*without the question of their being objectively true or false being raised at all.* In short, we have created a climate in which a thing's *seeming* to be true is often mistaken for its *being* true.

How have we done this? By stressing and distorting nonrational dimensions of believing. The best-known examples of this are from the field of psychology. It's common knowledge now that people have nonrational, psychological grounds for believing and disbelieving things. These psychological factors are behind the reasons they give for believing a particular thing and have nothing whatever to do with the belief's being objectively true or false. A particular belief merely seems true or seems false because of a psychological state of mind which wishes or fears it to be so.

Freud called attention to this as "rationalizing," and his well-known exposé of the technique threatened to uncover our work. What has saved us is that the category of rationalization has been applied so selectively, partly because of Freud's own bias. When believers wanted or needed their faith to be true, skeptics derided it as rationalizing. But when unbelievers wanted or needed faith to be untrue, the same skeptics, abandoning their skepticism, described it as tough-minded and applauded. In the shuffle, of course, we have conveniently obscured the fact that Christianity actually claims to *be* true.

Fortunately, people are less aware of sociological examples of the same thing. Again it was touch and go whether our cover might be blown; and, curiously, the person who has best understood the importance of the social dimension of believing is one of their own intelligence experts.[3] As he has seen correctly, the degree to which a belief (or disbelief) seems convincing is directly related to its "plausibility structure"—that is, the group or community which provides the social and psychological support for the belief. If the support structure is strong, it is easy to believe; if the support structure is weak, it is difficult to believe. The question of whether the group's belief is actually true or not may never become an issue.

You see, then, how our Parisian skepticism was more likely to *seem* true on the Left Bank than on the Right. On the Left Bank it was a whole, shared world, not just an intellectual idea. In the same way, Roman Catholicism is more likely to *seem* true in Eire than in Egypt, just as Mormonism is in Salt Lake City than in Singapore, and Marxism in Moscow than in Mecca. In each case, plausibility comes from a world of shared support. Coach it with care, and plausibility will upstage credibility. It then becomes for the belief not just a cradle but a crutch without which the believer would be stranded. This is why the Left Bank philosophy could never cross the Seine.

If this social dimension was vital in an intellectual milieu like the Left Bank (it is also true in Oxford, if you think about it), how much more will it be true in an area like Los Angeles, which puts such a premium on experience, relationships and atmospheres. Fortunately, although the clearest analysis of plausibility is by an enemy expert, his own side is likely to be the last to see it. Even that diminishing band of Christians still concerned to defend the faith are almost totally preoccupied with credibility (an intellectual problem) and have little concern for plausibility (a problem with social dimensions as well).

There is a double irony in this preoccupation. First, that the enemy, who is generally so resistant to thinking, has developed an intellectualist bias of any kind. Second, that they have gone overboard by being too theoretical even though the Adversary's warnings against this are clear. He himself is no stranger to the idea of "fleshing out" theory. His directive was always that faith be truth that is practiced (giving it the necessary social dimension) and not merely professed, propounded, proclaimed (or some other purely theoretical response). It was once hard work to break the hold of this idea in the church.

Even their inveterate theoretician Paul saw this point clearly. He knew it was the church, not theory, which was "the pillar and bulwark of the truth."[4] Of course he didn't mean that Christianity was true because the church was strong. He wasn't stupid; he was stubborn. He would have believed his faith was objectively true if he'd been the last one left convinced of it. But just as the Party is the plausibility structure for Marxism, and the Senior Common Room (or "faculty lounge" as you'll have to call it now) can be the same for secular humanism, the church is the plausibility structure for the Christian faith. Paul realized this. The church is Christianity's working model, its pilot plant, its future in embryo.

You can understand, then, our need to undermine Christianity through the church, not so much at the level of truth as at the level of plausibility. Uproot Christians physically from a well-functioning community or alienate them inwardly from a poorly functioning one, and the rest of our job will take care of itself. There is a French saying that the Breton peasant checks his faith at the left-luggage office in the Gare Montparnasse on arriving in Paris.[5] But the same is true of the student from a Christian home checking his faith at his first seminar, or of anyone changing worlds. On entering the new world, the old becomes implausible, and soon its faith becomes incredible too.

Irony apart, however, the church's preoccupation with credibility and neglect of plausibility is typical of her weakness. Without a feel for the social dimension of believing, the church is like a person paralyzed from the neck down—quite insensible to the further damage being inflicted on her.

## No Tool for Cultural Analysis
"If you want to know what water is, why is the fish the last one you ask?" runs the Chinese riddle. This captures the essential difficulty

that Christians have in becoming aware of their cultural context, and it is an excellent introduction to the second factor.

*Culture* understood as primitive African masks or the sexual habits of South Sea Islanders is easy for Christians to grasp. It's conveniently distant in time or space. But their own culture is quite different. It's the water in which they swim and the mold by which they're shaped, so it isn't easy for them to perceive. Culture is therefore a simple way to influence Christians without their realizing it.

In theory, cultural blindness should be less of a problem for Christians than for others. From their notion of worldliness you'd expect them to deduce that their allegiance does not operate in a vacuum, that the cultural context is never neutral, and that the worst dangers are often the least obvious. But then, of course, "the world," along with "the flesh and the devil," has been consigned today to the doctrinal attic. A most fortunate oversight.

An understanding of their cultural context should be a basic stock in trade for Christians. Such an awareness would affect not only their notion of worldliness and witnessing, but also their discipleship, theological self-understanding and ethical decision making. Occasional stirrings toward cultural analysis do occur from time to time, and in fact such a stirring is happening today. This might pose a serious threat to us, were it not for two things.

In the first place, the new Christian interest in cultural analysis is almost completely restricted to intellectuals. Under the pressure of the so-called knowledge industry (a pressure which these analysts have largely failed to analyze), there has been such a drive toward specialization that their own analyses are becoming more rarefied and less intelligible to ordinary people. Congresses, consultations, reports and papers are proliferating, and an impressive new jargon is emerging. Sophisticated talk of "evangelologists" and "missiological hermeneutics" is replacing tactless, old-fashioned phrases like "passion for the lost." But their mission is no more effective.

This flurry of cultural analysis will not cause us problems. We should even work *with* this trend, so that evangelism suffers the same fate as apologetics and becomes an almost purely theoretical exercise—well staffed and monitored by a growing band of missiological experts and theoreticians.

In addition, Christians are using tools of analysis which haven't got a hare's chance of detecting where our most damaging work is being done. As you know, in Christian circles today there are three main approaches to analyzing culture: the history of ideas, which traces the intellectual pedigree of thought; cultural anthropology, which interprets thought in the setting of human cultures and customs; and the sociology of knowledge, which interprets the impact of everyday experience on all that passes for knowledge. Fortunately, this last one, which would lead them straight to the heart of our Operation, they have almost completely overlooked.

Anyone stopping to think would see that all three approaches are necessary. They don't compete; they complement each other. But if one should be overlooked, far better for us that it be the third. It is the least used, but it would probably be the most useful for the church at the present moment.

If we can keep Christians beavering away on the other two approaches, they won't notice the limitations. Cultural anthropology may be a help in describing the less-developed world (or the "mission field" as they quaintly describe it), but is difficult to transfer to the modern world. Similarly, analyzing the history of ideas has its own shortcomings (it's impossible to understand intellectual history by sticking solely to intellectual ideas),[6] and it has practical difficulties. It is hard enough to do and harder still to make useful sense of to the average person. (After all, how do Kant, Hegel and Kierkegaard *really* influence the nine-to-five world of the exuberant Pentecostal in Buenos Aires or the staid Baptist in Brighton?)

It could be tricky for us, however, if they cotton to the sociology of knowledge.[7] It would present them with no such drawbacks. It deals with the modern world and insists on seeing it from the perspective of ordinary experience. Fortunately, the very name *sociology of knowledge* is enough to put most people off. And although the core idea is simple and practical, it can easily be surrounded with enough jargon to make it unintelligible. Keeping a smoke screen around the sociology of knowledge is crucial. Once Christians see it as a simple tool and begin to use it, our position is at risk. When people can trace a line from a thought to the thinker and then to the world in which the thought arose, they are halfway to seeing how ideas are influenced by their social contexts.

That is not to say that the sociology of knowledge would ever be a magic shortcut to easy understanding. On the contrary, several versions of it are like a minefield to faith, so a sudden rush by earnest Christians to rectify their ignorance could blow up in their faces. Yet the best current sociology of knowledge is only an elaboration on what the clearest Christian thinkers have seen all along: that truth seemingly "changes color as it changes climate," as Pascal put it.[8] That is the sort of analysis we dare not let them regain.

In some areas, the history of ideas is the tool they need anyway, so Christians can scrape by without using the sociology of knowledge. For example, if they stick to discussing theological doctrines, the history of ideas approach goes a long way. But not even theological doctrines are as pure as they think, and the degree to which social contexts play a part would surprise them.

Where their analysis comes badly unstuck is in areas where people's thinking is as much influenced by their ordinary experience as by theoretical ideas. Relying solely on the history of ideas in those areas is a self-imposed handicap. For instance, how might the average Christian explain what has influenced the modern concept of time?

"Aha!" he might rush to reply, as if brandishing his potted history of Western thought. "The modern view of time is linear and progressive and is a result of the biblical view of time as it has been interpreted by Augustine and reinterpreted by contemporary thinkers such as Einstein."

He'd be right, of course, up to a point. Yet what he would miss would be the far more basic and down-to-earth influences, such as those of clocks, watches, timetables, schedules, diaries and calendars. He'd overlook these because he'd think they're so obvious they're hardly worth attention. But there he is wrong. Much closer to the mark would be the old Filipino description of Westerners as "people with gods on their wrists." On your next advance trip, try out some local L.A. churches and observe how the Sunday sermon comes to a hasty close as a chorus of digital alarms goes off at noon. It's not just ideas that form their view of time nor just the Bible that makes them tick.

Do you know Jean François Millet's painting *The Angelus*?[9] As the sun sets and the Angelus rings out, two peasants stop and bow reverently amidst their work in the fields. You couldn't have a greater contrast than with your modern digital chorus. With one, "Christian time" is breaking into the world of work; with the other, "secular time" is breaking into the world of worship. The Angelus and the Angelenos are a universe apart, and most Christians would never know why.

In other areas, the history of ideas has little or nothing to say, so many Christians are hopelessly at sea. Take certain mundane but hardly inconsequential areas which we have been monitoring, such as the rise of the drive-in church ("Come as you are—in the family car"). It would be futile to try to analyze such four-wheel fellowship solely from the history of ideas. Some nimble interpreters might claim to "discover" that all along the Adversary's handbook should have read, "Praise God in the chariot!" But they would miss the obvious point: a culture of mobility plus convenience—Los Angeles par excellence—leads quite naturally not only to drive-in theaters and banks, but to drive-in churches. Driving-in is as natural as breathing to your future fellow citizens. Many of the L.A. churches are really commuter fellowships. Walking to church only means walking from the parking lot.

Our opportunity lies in the words *leads naturally*. These may be tiny examples, but overlay upon overlay, the effect in molding lives is radical. Thus the slow, subtle but all-powerful shaping of culture has all the advantages of a complete philosophical revolution with none of the disadvantages of intellectual sweat.

Curiously, that is not the end. If most Christians are oblivious to the advantages of using the sociology of knowledge, others are obtuse about it. They reject it, claiming to know what it is, when often they have the wrong end of the stick. Their misconceptions are equally to our advantage. The crude, one-dimensional efforts of certain Marxists to claim the tool as their own have been especially helpful in maintaining our smoke screen. The result of their blundering is that, even where it is known, the whole enterprise is tainted with the suspicion that it is incurably deterministic, reductionist and debunking.

That suits us down to the ground. "If you can't deny it, distort it" has always been a favorite maxim of ours. Without a proper grasp of the tool of the sociology of knowledge, it is highly unlikely that Christians will detect our work before it is too late. Some enemy analysts have recently succeeded in drumming into their people's minds, "As a man thinks, so he is." That in itself will not disturb the Operation. But it is absolutely essential that the true relationship of thought and culture as a two-way conversation (dialectical and not determinist, as it's put technically) remain well obscured.

**No Skill at Contemporary Comment**
If the first two factors were not enough, this last one clinches the matter for us. The chances of Christians developing a feel for the social dimension of belief and acquiring a new tool for cultural analysis are extremely small. But even if they did, a third factor makes it almost certain that attempts to detect and describe our Operation would be ineffective: They have no skill in contemporary cultural comment. This is true in the present situation, in which such attempts are rare, and it should hold true for any future situation in which cultural awareness increases dramatically.

What we can always count on to create confusion are the age-old pitfalls of intelligence gathering which beset cultural analysis too; for what intelligence gathering is to the state, cultural analysis is to the church. All intelligence work is dogged by the problem of distorting factors. (For example, inter-departmental rivalries or the unreliability of irregular or personal reporting sources—what U.S. intelligence jargon calls "old boy channels.") What we must do with the church is to make such distortions acceptable as unavoidable risks. Their cultural comment will then be based on faulty analysis, making it either worthless or damaging.

The first type of faulty cultural analysis involves a distortion in *description.* Modern Christians often presume that, because they are modern, they know what their modern context is. That entirely false presumption is bred into them partly by their familiarity with their culture ("If *we* don't know our own culture, who does?") and partly by its all-embracing character (it's the water in which they swim).

The truth is that, like everyone else, *Christians are always more culturally shortsighted than they realize.* They are often unable to tell, for instance, where their Christian principles leave off and cultural perspectives begin. Among other things, this means that it is easy for us to keep the church hopping between inflated pronouncements marked by an absence of cultural awareness and hand-wringing humility that is obsessed with it. I'll show you examples of this as we proceed. But for the moment simply note that conservative-minded Christians are especially prone to the former (an absence of cultural awareness), just as liberal-minded ones are prone to the latter (an obsession with cultural constraints).

The next time you go to L.A. and find yourself waiting in a barbershop, leaf through a few old magazines covering presidential elections. Look for descriptions of America's "Christian past" or for the "morality indexes" by which conservatives were urged to judge the voting record of senators and representatives. The confusion of Christian principles and conservative politics was priceless, and it will be a key to their undoing.

Curiously, both the conservative-minded and the liberal-minded confuse Christian convictions and cultural conditioning, although in opposite ways. The extreme conservatives are unaware of the problem of conditioning. They raise their culture to the level of their convictions and claim too much for it, absolutizing and defending it blindly with a devotion proper to their faith. Their economics is as holy as their ark.

Not to be outdone, the extreme liberals do the reverse. Aware of little else than the problem of conditioning, they lower their convictions to the level of their culture. They therefore claim too little for them, relativizing and dismissing them blithely with a nonchalance proper to their culture. Their ark is as humdrum as their everyday world.

The net effect is pure enchantment. The conservatives allow their culture to swagger around with the authority of their Christian convictions, while the liberals allow their Christian convictions to be swallowed alive by culture. The wilder we can make these extremes, the more each will refuel the swing to the other and make the problem self-perpetuating.

A second type of faulty analysis involves a distortion in *evaluation*. The distinction between description and evaluation is not hard and fast, of course (even in science), but it is important. Let me illustrate. One evening, after dining at one of the Oxford colleges, Lord Nuffield was surprised at the porter's accurate memory in handing him his hat. "How did you know it was mine?" he asked.

The porter replied, "I didn't, Sir! All I knew was that it was the one you came in with!" Such a cool and judicious refusal to make judgments that go beyond the evidence is exactly what is rare among Christians today. There is more than one way by which they stumble into bad judgment.

To begin with, most Christians simply haven't developed Christian tools of analysis to examine culture properly. Or rather, the tools the church once had have grown rusty or been mislaid. What often happens is that Christians wake up to some incident or issue and suddenly realize they need to analyze what's going on. Then, having no tools of their own, they lean across and borrow the tools nearest them.

They don't realize that, in their haste, they are borrowing not an isolated tool but a whole philosophical toolbox laden with tools which have their own particular bias to every problem (a Trojan horse in the toolbox, if you like). The toolbox may be Freudian, Hindu or Marxist. Occasionally, the toolbox is right-wing; more often today it is liberal or left-wing (the former mainly in North

America, the latter mainly in Europe). Rarely—and this is all that matters to us—is it consistently or coherently Christian.

When Christians use tools for analysis (or bandy certain terms of description) which have non-Christian assumptions embedded within them, these tools (and terms) eventually act back on them like wearing someone else's glasses or walking in someone else's shoes. The tools shape the user. Their recent failure to think critically about culture has made Christians uniquely susceptible to this.

Again, I'll show you plenty of examples of this as we proceed. Here is a simple illustration. Extreme liberalism's susceptibility to fashion is proverbial, but now we are achieving the same success with certain younger conservatives; for instance, in the current rage in Britain for the "prophetic" stance. In the modern secular world older conservative Christians have been widely disinherited by the establishment to which they had been uncomplaining chaplains for so long. Not satisfied with the "purely spiritual" role of their parents, many younger conservatives are casting around furiously for stances that are prophetic. They are thus an easy prey for one of our simplest delusions: For those who aspire to be prophets, the first task is to attack the foremost temptation.

The truth is that the foremost temptation is usually yesterday's. That's why it's obvious. Thus our young turks have often only seen the problems today (middle-class hypocrisy, patriotic jingoism and so on) because these are no longer today's central problems. In Britain, at least. Such prophetic chic serves us as well as any priestly compliance which preceded it. Indeed, prophetic chic could be the beginning of a new priestly compliance to a new set of ideas and identifications. Once such young conservatives were silent; now they are strident. But of course, changing from a middle-class stance to an anti-middle-class stance is no more the origin of a prophetic calling than doing the reverse.

What many of them fail to ask themselves as they speak is: Where are they coming from? What is their context? (questions that demand critical self-evaluation). Blindness in that area was always the mark of the most successful false prophets. Today's junior Jere-miahs and aspiring Amoses are no problem to us, especially if they confine themselves to pulpit rhetoric and windy editorializing. Like a bomb with a faulty timing device, such delayed-action prophecy harms no one but themselves.

Christians who don't carelessly ignore the nature of their assumptions often make the opposite mistake. They crudely impose their assumptions on everyone and everything, too woodenly and too soon. In this way they leap to false conclusions before they discover what is going on, and they judge people before they've properly heard them. That is the main reason why Christian judgments are often so hasty and inaccurate and why, instead of being prophetic, Christians often come across to the world as needlessly provocative or just plain comic. Horrified by "cheap grace," many Christians are backing happily into its opposite—cheap judgment.

Among other types of faulty cultural analysis, perhaps the best one to encourage is distortion through *generalization*. There are numerous ways this can occur. The most common is when definite but scanty evidence is inflated beyond all recognition. Let our generalizing Christian talk to one Sydney taxi driver, and before long he will be fulminating on "what the Australians believe." Or let her pick up one California hitchhiker, and she will be an authority on the "new religious consciousness." Or let him read some wishful description of the religionless era, and his talk for months will be heavy with references to "the coming of age of modern man."

This mythical "modern man" is their most useful ventriloquist's dummy. It can be made the mouthpiece for all the generalizer's opinions, the alibi for his lack of evidence. Such talk is not only sloppy; it is usually hopelessly wrong at some key point, and it is always to be cultivated.

Our strong suit here is that, however expert and careful Christians are in their own fields, it is impossible for them to become expert everywhere. In any case, their ranks have been so thinned by lack of thinking over the last century that they are struggling on several fronts at once. The result is that as soon as they leave the territory of their own expertise (as a lawyer or theologian or what-ever), they are bound to stray into areas they know less well and be-come amateur sociologists unawares (or amateur psychologists, lawyers, theologians or whatever). As soon as they do that, they make themselves sitting ducks.

Take the example of the *Honest to God* debate. It would be instruc-tive for you to trace the use of the word *secularization*. It was repeated endlessly like a mantra and flourished as an "open sesame" that would unlock the stored riches of the new theological thinking. Only later did it dawn on a short-changed intellectual public that none of the theologians who used the word gave it a critical definition, and none had adopted a formal definition from the field where the de-bate arose.[10] As one Frenchman observed after reading such theo-logical pronouncements: It is difficult to decide whether the writer is stating a fact, making a cultural observation, painting an imagi-nary picture or merely expressing a wish.[11]

### Not Only in California
I need not say more about these three main factors. Together they produce the sandman effect and create a state of almost total de-fenselessness and vulnerability. In terms of her alertness to cultural danger, the church is virtually in a coma.

I must return to your original point, however, and end with a note of caution. We would be piling irony upon irony if our strategy, which is built on subverting strength, were itself subverted at its strongest point. Subversion works best when the process is slow and subtle. It must never be recognizable until it is irreversible. This means that all sectors of the modern church are to be subverted at once, although obviously in different ways and at somewhat dif-ferent speeds. The situation must never arise in which the cultural subversion of one sector becomes so obvious that it acts as an alarm to rouse the rest of the church.

You must take special note of this. The danger is particularly strong in areas like Los Angeles where the local culture is so power-ful and coercive. Your temptation will be to confuse *extreme* with *effective,* and so to overplay your hand and give the game away. Strictly between us, this was precisely the mistake made by your predecessor, and the reason why he was "promoted" to another region. Had it not been for the prompt intervention of the Disinformation Department, our whole Operation might have been in jeopardy. As parts of the church began to stir, Disinformation covered his excesses by soothingly repeating, "Only in California ... it could only happen in California...."

The fact is that we are making the church captive not only in California but all around the modern world. For lasting results, remember finesse. Subtle compromise is always better than sudden captivity. See that their dreams are undisturbed.

# MEMORANDUM
## 3

**SUBJECT:**

# THE CHESHIRE-CAT FACTOR

**FROM:**
DEPUTY DIRECTOR,
CENTRAL SECURITY COUNCIL
**TO:**
DIRECTOR DESIGNATE,
LOS ANGELES BUREAU
**CLASSIFICATION:**
ULTRA SECRET

■

Have you acquired a taste for Lewis Carroll while you've been in Oxford? He couldn't be more different from the French writers I was working with, but I quite enjoy him for light reading. At any rate, you will remember his celebrated Cheshire cat and the giddying effect it had on Alice. Slowly, beginning with the end of its tail, the cat began to vanish until there was nothing left except the grin, which remained some time after the rest of it had gone.

"Well," thought Alice in surprise, "I've often seen a cat without a grin, but a grin without a cat! It's the most curious thing I saw in my life!"

That is an excellent picture of our success in subverting the modern church. Unlike the Cheshire cat, however, the church is not vanishing of its own accord and cannot reappear at will. Think of it. Less than three centuries since our Operation began, and we have drained the life out of the church. Where it has not vanished entirely, what is left is little more than an empty, lingering grin— empty, certainly, by contrast with what it was before.

Look, for example, at "Christian Europe." For five centuries the history of the world has virtually been European history, and whoever rules the world of tomorrow will rule a world pried loose from its own traditional past by European ideas, European tools and European precedents. Yet as André Malraux says, "The death of Europe is the central fact of our time."[1] Do you think it is only a coincidence that the death of Europe follows so closely upon the stilling of the faith which was its heartbeat?

From Scandinavia to the Mediterranean and from the Atlantic to the Urals, the dawning of the modern world in Europe has reduced the church to a condition which, measured by its former standards, is one of virtual collapse. Even in countries like England, shaped unmistakably by centuries of reformation and renewal, fewer than one adult in ten attends church each week.[2]

Or look at the United States, that super-Europe or Europe-across-the-water. The picture of Christian faith and practice there looks better at first glance. In areas like the Midwest roughly three-quarters of the population are church members.[3] But a closer look suggests that the coming of the modern world to America has led to a vital change in the Christian faith.

The same historic words are said and sung, but what is shown tells a different story. The indicators of faith are still up (buoyant numbers, increased giving, high spiritual interest and so on), but contrary to the popular impression, the impact of faith on moral, social and political life is diminishing, as we shall see. One out of every three Americans now claims to have been "born again," yet American life goes on much as before.

It may be true that there are more Christians in America than ever before and that they have never had so much money at their disposal, such powerful technologies to use, such positions of influence to fill, or such a global opportunity to which to respond. But the signs are that the opportunity will be squandered and that much of American Christendom is more modern and more American than it is decisively Christian.

Imagine showing the church of today to the Christian of yesterday, to the apostle Paul, for example, or Augustine, Calvin or Pascal. They would rub their eyes in disbelief. Compared with the solid body of the thing they knew, what's left of the church, as one of her present agents laments, is little more than a "disembodied wraith."[4]

I will explain here how we have reached the present situation and how we can exploit it to the full. But keep in the back of your mind that the Cheshire-cat factor is only the first of three pressures which we have brought to bear on the church. You will appreciate the full extent of the damage when you can stand back and survey the impact of all three pressures together.

This first pressure happens to be the most important, since it is the earliest and most basic. But it is also unquestionably the hardest to grasp. It's not quick to reveal its secrets, but master it because it is breathtaking when you understand it.

### The Heart of the Matter

The technical term for the Cheshire-cat factor is *secularization*. This has been defined in a host of conflicting ways, many of which can be traced back to the superb confusion sown by the Department of Disinformation. But we must never succumb to our own propaganda, so it is important to keep the proper definition clearly in mind.

By secularization I mean *the process through which, starting from the center and moving outward, successive sectors of society and culture have been freed from the decisive influence of religious ideas and institutions.*[5] In other words, secularization is the process by which we have neutralized the social and cultural significance of religion in the central areas of modern society, such as the worlds of science, technology, bureaucracy and so on, *making religious ideas less meaningful and religious institutions more marginal.* Our goals in this are simple: to negate worship and to neutralize the Adversary's rule.

I realize that this definition begs a number of key questions, but let me leave them on one side for the moment and turn to a most extraordinary fact. Since 1900 the percentage of the world's atheistic and nonreligious peoples (agnostics, materialists, Communists and so on) has grown from 0.2 per cent to 21.3 per cent; in other words, from a mere one-fifth of one per cent to over one fifth of the world's population.[6]

This is the most dramatic change on the entire religious map of the twentieth century. Even Christian findings affirm this now, although the gloomiest of Christian prophets didn't foresee such a possibility in 1900. Atheistic and nonreligious peoples now form the second largest bloc in the world, second only to Christians and catching up with them fast. (Eight and a half million "converts" each year to be precise. If they continue to multiply at the same rate, they'll reach one billion by the much-dreaded year 1984.[7] How's that for a statistic to embellish some new conspiracy theory?)

"Come now," you may be saying. "You can't take credit for that. That success is due to the improved performance of the Counter-Apologetics Division. All you are describing is the dramatic rise in secular alternatives to religious belief."

In one way, you would be quite correct, but that distorts the true picture of what has happened. As I have defined it, secularization is not the same thing as secularism, so it cannot be measured by a Dow Jones index of rising or falling atheism.

*Secularism* is a philosophy and has all the strengths and weaknesses of one, not least that to subscribe to it usually demands some effort of mind or will. *Secularization,* by contrast, is not a philosophy; it's a process. More important still, its roots are not in an intellectual concept but in institutional change. It's a process which has actually taken place in the structures of society. Secularization has its subjective and its intellectual side—what might be called modern consciousness or the modern mentality—but this is the result and not the root of the process.

Unlike a philosophy, this mentality is not something people think about or choose. Rather, it rubs off on them. It comes as part and parcel of objective, institutional changes which have actually occurred through modernization and cannot be avoided or simply wished away. Secularization is therefore contagious in a way that secularism never is. Wherever modernization goes, some degree of infection is inevitable.

On the other hand, although secularization is not the same thing as secularism, it promotes and improves on the old weapon in two important ways: it goes deeper and reaches further. Secularization (the process) goes deeper in that *it provides the perfect setting for secularism* (the philosophy). Imagine a sports shop in a ski resort that wants to improve its sale of ski wear. What would help it most would be to have not only attractive designs, but also good snow conditions. Even the best designs would sell poorly in the Sahara. Similarly, secularization provides the perfect conditions for secularism. It's the new context which enhances the old concept, making the latter seem natural, even necessary.

Therefore, with due respect to the excellence of your counter-apologists, they cannot take credit for the recent surge of secularism. We've had secularism around for millenia, but it has never before caught on like this, because it lacked the ideal conditions. Look at nineteenth-century skepticism, either in England or on the Continent. When it stuck to largely intellectual arguments, as the secularist societies did, it appealed to only a tiny minority. But when it caught the imagination of the masses through other means, people were converted without any serious argument or extensive reading. The soil was well prepared. As one enemy historian notes, secularism and secularization are not the same problem. "Enlightenment was of the few. Secularization is of the many."[8]

Up to the nineteenth century, discussion of religion had been continued in roughly the same context for thousands of years. An intelligent Roman would have been as much at home discussing Christianity with Pascal or Voltaire as with his contemporaries. But today's conditions would amaze them all. The truth is, a whole gamut of things has gone into the breeding of all these recent agnostics and materialists, including in the Eastern bloc some old-fashioned persuasion, KGB-style. But in all of it, argument has played the lesser role and atmosphere the greater. The contribution of secularization has been decisive.

In addition, secularization reaches further than secularism in that *it affects and influences religious people too.* Since it is a silent process which has happened rather than a philosophy which can be chosen or rejected, it subtly shapes those people (Christians included) who would never knowingly subscribe to such a philosophy and turns them into subconscious secularists. Engels noted wryly how English religion and respectability were infected by nineteenth-century skepticism: "The introduction of salad oil has been accompanied by a fateful spread of Continental scepticism in matters religious."[9] But secularization today has come under a more sophisticated cover and is far more devastating.

Thus, secularization works for us because of a double thrust: *it compounds secularism,* thereby increasing its power, but *it also constricts religion,* thereby decreasing the power of religion. Both secularization and secularism have the same destination, but secularization is the stronger, surer, subtler means of reaching it.

I have said more about what secularization isn't than about what it is. But one further point before we explore the latter. As you will have recognized, this use of secularization as a weapon marks a definite departure from our usual tactics. For the first time, we will appear to attack not only the Christian faith, but other religions in the modern world. In other words, as part of our movement against Christianity in particular, we will use secularization to subvert religion in general.

Some of the old guard on the Council saw this as unnecessarily hazardous. After all, it's been a standard operating principle that bad religion is far more damaging to true faith than no religion. Generally speaking, this still holds true. But bear in mind certain things about Operation Gravedigger. In the first place, it is more than just another operation. If it succeeds, the Western church will be in our pocket, and it will be the curtain-raiser to the final thrust for victory over the church worldwide.

In addition, secularization will never be total or permanent, whatever certain theologians claim. The belief that it will is an illusion which springs from a succession of conceits. These thinkers have turned their backs on an older, more explicit conceit ("Christianity and civilization are one") and even on its more implicit, modern form ("The collapse of the West is the end of the world"). But they've fallen for the subtlest conceit ("The decline of the church means the disappearance of all religion").

The fact is that the present moment of maximum secularization is only an interim period between the passing of the Christian age and the rise of a new religious era. Theologians may talk of secularization as "exorcism," but only because of the secularization of their own theology. No one will be more dismayed by the number of new gods and old ghosts which crowd in as squatters in the conveniently emptied house.

Also, remember that we are promoting secularization not to remove Christianity altogether, but to *reduce its influence in areas essential to its integrity and effectiveness.* By putting an end to Christian influence in the central sectors of modern society, we contradict the Adversary's claim to authority over the *whole* of his followers' lives. Once that is done, what faith they have left will be inconsequential and will lack the mental or moral muscle to resist us. In fact, once domesticated, such faith will be a useful workhorse for the society we have in mind. The "pit pony" of tomorrow's world, as the Director likes to say.

**Something New under the Sun**
Field agents who have never served anywhere but on the modern front do not appreciate the magnitude of what's been done. If you telescope the last three centuries, what we have achieved is little short of revolutionary, but latecomers take it as routine and miss its significance. Our progress becomes easily apparent if you compare the situation we have engineered with what was typical in the past.

For example, compare the state of Christianity in twentieth-century Europe or America with that in the nineteenth, eighteenth, seventeenth or sixteenth centuries. The numbers of Christians in these earlier times might have varied, spiritual vitality might have ebbed or flowed, and compromise and hypocrisy might at times have been more evident than fidelity. But where there was faith, however small numerically, it had a characteristic social and cultural influence because it mulishly insisted on applying the Adversary's rule to all of life. "If Jesus Christ is not lord of all, he is not lord at all" could have been the banner under which the faithful soldiered. Modern faith, however large it is in numbers (as in America), almost never has this total view. It is secularization which has made the difference.

Or think more generally of how human beings have always been open to a world beyond the world of the natural, visible and tangible.[10] Certainly most people spent most of their lives in the "seven-to-eleven waking world" of mundane, everyday concerns and interests. Certainly there were varying degrees of openness to anything beyond, with most people fitting comfortably between the extremes of skeptic and mystic. Certainly many of the experiences that went beyond ordinary reality (for example dreams) were not necessarily considered to be religious.

Nevertheless, the deepest experiences of all were held to be "religious," "sacred," "other" or "transcendent," however these terms were defined. These experiences called ordinary life into question and cast a religious frame of meaning around the everyday world. Pursuits as down-to-earth as business deals, making love, farming and politics were all seen in the light of the world beyond. Human worlds had to creep in for shelter under the shade of divine truth.

Secularization has changed all that. Today, for some people all of the time, and for most people some of the time, secularization ensures that ordinary reality is not just the official reality, but the only reality.

Human life has traditionally been lived in a house with windows to other worlds. These windows may have sometimes become dirty, broken or boarded up, but they were always there. Only in the modern world have we achieved what has been called "a world without windows."[11] Shut off from transcendence, modern people are shut up to triviality.

Once you see this, you get a very different perspective on the exaggerated talk of a new religious consciousness in the West or of an explosion of Christian growth around the world. It's happening in one sense, but at the moment it's paltry stuff compared with the expansion of the new secular consciousness.

In the Soviet Union, for example, the percentage of people who identify themselves as Christians has dropped from 83.6 per cent in 1900 to 36.1 per cent today.[12] "With a little help from our KGB friends," you say? The picture in Western Europe and America is hardly different. Defections from the Christian faith in the "free West" are now rising at the rate of 1,820,500 former Christians a year or 7,600 church attenders daily.[13] In other words, the losses more than outweigh all the church's gains (even in Africa and Asia). The picture is equally gratifying in terms of those who still claim to believe. In the United Church of Canada, for example, less than half the members profess an unequivocal belief in God.[14]

This pattern of defection is true both in terms of statistics (Christianity's share of the world's population is shrinking) and significance (Christian gains are all in the premodern world, Christian losses in the modern). To return to my picture of the sports shop, you could put it like this. If secularization provides inviting snow conditions and tempts people to buy a new ski outfit, it makes religious beliefs seem as unseasonal as swimwear in a blizzard. Religious swimwear may be part of the après-ski world, but it is distinctly chilly and uninviting for the rugged slopes of the real world.

The present irrelevance of religion is unique in human history, an achievement we owe mainly to secularization.

**The Blowout and the Fallout**
I'd be intrigued to know what you had already glimpsed of the Cheshire-cat factor. Some agents kick themselves when it is first explained. The thing had been going on right before their eyes, but

they had been trying to interpret it in overly intellectual frameworks which ignore cultural infiltration and concentrate on concepts rather than context.

You won't have made that mistake, but a precise mind like yours will want to get down to more than a general definition of secularization in terms of its character, causes and long-term results. You'll also need to examine the overall process of modernization which has carried this secularizing effect.

Keep in the back of your mind that secularization is not produced by any one cause. This is the secret of its elusiveness and power. The fact that it cannot be traced to any single cause works to our advantage in various ways. Enemy analysts sometimes hunt for a clear explanation that can be verified with scientific precision. Failing to find it, they pronounce the search impossible or the danger a hoax. We're eternally indebted to them for diverting people's attention from the problem.

Other intelligence experts, determined to be less simplistic, seek to account for the secularizing effect with a complex chain of causes and subtle reasoning. Obviously we have to keep track of their work much more closely; there is always a slight chance they could break through to a correct understanding. But the reality is terrribly slippery. Often as a result, their complications thicken, their subtleties grow more and more refined, the number of their variable factors slowly mounts, while the explanation grows more elusive still. In the end, the search becomes a goal in itself. The fox escapes, but the excitement of the chase is strong, and the hunt goes on and on.

The top field agents who will return to the Summer Training Seminars this year will have a course on the full complexity of the dynamics of secularization. But here I want simply to draw your attention to the two most important trends behind it. These are only two of many trends which could be cited, and secularization cannot be traced back to either of them in a single, straight line. Yet these trends are fundamental, and their contribution to secularization is like the combined effect of a volcanic explosion and the fallout of acid rain.

*1. The displacement of religion.*    Have you ever seen a silhouette of the London skyline in the eighteenth century? Compare it with the same skyline today. The contrast in Paris is equally striking. What is dramatic about the earlier skylines is the dominance of church architecture. Abbeys and cathedrals tower above the other buildings, representing the social power of the church, while spires and steeples, symbolizing the human spirit, thrust upward to a world beyond.

Today, by contrast, the churches are dwarfed by skyscraping office blocks and crouch down somewhere between the banks and insurance buildings, cramped and overshadowed by a host of competing institutions.

Here is a vivid picture of the effect of the first trend: the movement in modernization toward *explosive diversification.* As modernization gathers speed and the rate of change quickens, the scale and complexity of institutions and ideas continue to mount. The result is a volcanic explosion of diversification. Specialized, separate areas are thrown up, each with its own premises, its own priorities and procedures—in a word, its own autonomy.

You can see this process most clearly on a physical level. Between 1861 and 1905, for example, the population of Paris grew by nearly 100 per cent, but the number of parishes grew by only 33 per cent and the number of priests by about 30 per cent.[15] Statistics for London show a similar picture. The churches were neither ready nor able to cope with the explosion.

I was reminded of this almost daily living in France. There is no more striking sight in the environs of Paris and other cities than the little church, intended for a village but now feebly serving a sprawling urban area. Inadequate in itself, it is marooned from the main currents of modern life and left to its own irrelevance.

I am not suggesting that secularization was a result of the collapse of the parish system. But the failure of the old parishes to deal with the new population was a symptom of the church's failure to keep up with the explosive diversification on all levels. Whole sectors of activity (such as the place of work) and whole segments of the population (such as the poor and the working class) were wrenched out of the control and concern of the church. The coziness of the traditional world, with its geographical concentration, social integration and conservative thought, was gone for good. The slums of the new cities were a symbol of Christian failure on a physical level. But a score of other equally uncared-for areas of thought and life were a sign that most Christians had been swept away by the explosion of modernity and had given up the unequal struggle to keep abreast.

Thus, modern work and the modern working class were both born in a century when traditional Christianity was largely absent from the center of the stage.[16] Other ideologies were not so reticent, but despite the social and theoretical reverberations from this failure the church has not pulled itself together to regain the ground.

This process of explosive diversification has a secularizing effect on religion which is felt as *displacement*. Once the lava has settled, society's structural shape has changed beyond recognition. Religion no longer presides over much of society as it did in the past nor participates in all of life as the Christian faith is required to do. As a result, Christian institutions and ideas are displaced from the center of modern society and relegated to the margins. At one stroke, discipleship, in the sense of the Adversary's claim to rule over the whole spectrum of life, has been effectively neutralized.

*2. The disenchantment of religion.* As a useful introduction to this second trend, consider the growing alarm about acid rain. Borne on the shifting winds of expanding industrialization, acid rain is becoming a problem of planetary dimensions. A leisurely but lethal atmospheric plague, it brings silent devastation not only to lakes, forests and wildlife, but to the world's great buildings and statues.

Secularization is the acid rain of the spirit, the atmospheric cancer of the mind and the imagination. Vented into the air not only by industrial chimneys but by computer terminals, marketing techniques and management insights, it is washed down shower by shower, the deadliest destroyer of religious life the world has ever seen.

Consider for a moment what was involved in the Apollo moon

landing in 1969. No operation could be more characteristically modern, yet it was really no different in principle from designing a car or marketing a perfume. Strip away the awesomeness of the vision and the pride of achievement and what remains? A vast assembly of plans and procedures, all carefully calculated and minutely controlled, in which *nothing is left to chance*. By the same token, *nothing is left to human spontaneity or divine intervention*.

This is typical of the acid rain effect of the second trend: the modern movement toward *extensive rationalization*. Far from being an incidental consequence of modernization, this is one of its essential characteristics.

As modernization drives forward, more and more of what was formerly left to God or human initiative or the processes of nature is classified, calculated and controlled by the use of reason. This is not a matter of philosophical rationalism but of functional rationality. In other words, reason used for practical rather than theoretical ends; reason as the servant of technology and development rather than of theology and philosophy.

Notice once again that as modernization expands, so also does that portion of life which is covered and controlled by the systematic application of reason and technique. "Simply figure it out," says the engineer. "Anything can be made." "Simply figure it out," says the salesman. "Anything can be marketed." In other words, the systematic application of reason is seen as the best tool for mastering reality, and this movement of extensive rationalization is at the heart of the imperialistic spread of science and technology.

Check for yourself. You can now find how-to manuals not only for running factories and repairing cars, but for making love, converting souls and restyling your personality, all in five easy lessons. The evangelistic training manual and the Industrial Revolution may seem poles apart, but the former is only the latter writ small. Look closely at its style and its assumptions. Under the regimental control of reason and technique, wisdom has been reduced to know-how, fruitfulness to skill, and an arduous apprenticeship under a master to a breezy weekend seminar from an expert.

The overall result? If the impact of the *exploding diversification* is felt as *displacement,* with Christian institutions forced to become more marginal in modern society, then the impact of the *extending rationalization* is felt as *disenchantment,* and Christian ideas are forced to become less meaningful in modern society.

By disenchantment I mean simply that, as the controlling hand of practical reason stretches further and further, all the "magic and mystery" of life are reduced and removed. When reason has harnessed all the facts, figures and forces, divine intervention is as unwelcome as accident, divine law as antiquated as the divine right of kings. Human spontaneity becomes "the human factor," the weak link in the chain of procedures. Wonder, along with humility and notions about the sanctity of things, is totally out of place. Problem solving, twentieth-century style, is a matter of working Rubik's cube rather than unlocking the riddle of the universe.

Do you see how this has a secularizing effect? Medieval Christians could have as their maxim, "I dress their wounds, but God heals them." But how many modern Christians doing agricultural service in Africa would think of saying, "I irrigated the desert, but God made it grow"? The problem for the Christian in the modern world is not that practical reason is irreligious, but that in more and more areas of life religion is practically irrelevant. Total indifference to religion is characteristic of the central and expanding areas of modern life. The deadly rain has fallen and all the spiritual life it falls on is dead, stunted or deformed.

I said earlier that our goals were to neutralize discipleship and negate worship. The first is easy. Not all Christians enter the central areas of modern society, but all who do are constricted by secularization, even if unawares. Secularization therefore affects far more than the overt secularist; it touches the most spiritual people too.

Today only the young hothead still attempts to carry faith out into the secular world. Most believers are as used to being frisked by secular society's reality guards as they are to being checked for weapons on boarding an aircraft, so the chances of Christians taking over any modern society are accordingly reduced to zero.

Some Christians half realize that this has happened, but they don't fully appreciate what it means. Other Christians are themselves the best testimonies to our success. The founder of McDonald's hamburgers, for example, was recently quoted as saying, "I speak of faith in McDonald's as if it were a religion. I believe in God, family and McDonald's—*and in the office that order is reversed.*"[17] Our own

Propaganda Department couldn't have put it better.

Our second goal, negating worship, is more difficult to achieve. This is partly because the setting of worship lies outside the central and more secularized areas of society and partly because some people seek compensation in worship for secularization in work. They hunger for an overwhelming sense of transcendence in worship to make up for a distinctly underwhelming sense of triviality in work.

In an increasing number of cases, however, secularization from the central areas has spilled over even into worship. Take the conservative preoccupation with church growth and outreach or the liberal rage for cultural relevance (read Saturday's newspaper and you have Sunday's liturgy). Or go back to your local congregations with the digital alarms and busy minds. With pressures and priorities like theirs, the last thing they can afford is to be "lost in wonder, love, and praise." Their minds as well as their watches are synchronized with the "real world." Securely earthed in day-to-day life, not for a moment are they in danger of being "heavened." Worship in any depth is negated.

**Differences in Distribution**
What I have outlined so far are the basic aspects of secularization. Never minimize these, for wherever modernization spreads, certain effects can almost be guaranteed. For example, churches will not flourish in areas dominated by heavy industry; they will flourish even less if the area concerned is also working-class; and as cities grow bigger, churchgoing will continue to drop. Exceptions to such findings are rare.

Nevertheless, don't be misled into a simplistic equation of industrialization and loss of faith and assume that secularization will be uniform as well as universal in the modern world. That sort of conclusion is common, but wrong. So let me describe where secularization is most likely to occur and how its fallout is likely to be distributed.[18]

Look first at the *central sectors* of modern society: the worlds of science, technology, bureaucracy, most business, most politics, most education and so on—the "real world" as they put it. Here is where you will find faith most irrelevant and secularization closest to being universal and uniform, even though thousands of religious people may service this area. Here is the heartland of the modern world, the quarter where the changes are most complete and where it is most obvious that diversification has led to the displacement of religion and rationalization to the disenchantment of religion.

The central sector is where the carriers of modernization are located (things such as technological innovation, the capitalist market economy and bureaucratic organization), so not surprisingly it is the sector most infected by secularization. To put it differently, it forms a sort of "no-go" area where the rule and relevance of religion are strictly excluded even for the most religious people. This is not, I emphasize again, because of any philosophic hostility, but because of the practical irrelevance of religion here. Religion in the no-go area is inadmissible, not because it is illegal but because it is considered inapplicable.

You know that since World War 2 the Soviet Union has recognized Japan as within the U.S. "sphere of influence"; and the U.S. in turn has recognized Eastern Europe as within the Soviet sphere. In much the same way, Christians have come to a tacit recognition that the central sectors of society are outside the "sphere of influence" of religion. This is quite contrary, of course, to their official party line. More importantly, from our point of view this no-go area is liberated territory, and it is expanding. Through winning it, we make nonsense of the Adversary's claim to total sovereignty over every inch of his people's lives.

The central sectors, however, are not the whole of society. Look next, therefore, at the carry-over of modernization into *less-central* sectors. These sectors are modern in a loose sense (they exist in the modern age), but they are less modern in a strict sense (they are less dominated by the principles and procedures of the modern sector). Among important elements in this less-modernized sector (which coincides roughly with the world outside work) are the family, leisure pursuits and, of course, the church.

When I speak of the central sector of modern society, all I have said about the basic processes of secularization is likely to apply and will need little qualification. But when I speak of the less-central sectors, the carry-over will not be automatic or complete. So make sure your understanding of the basic processes is balanced by an understanding of the different ways secularization is distributed. Just as acid rain is carried by the shifting winds, secularization carries over and reaches into other, more marginal areas of life according to social, spiritual and regional differences in each culture.

To put it simply, secularization would tend to occur along universal and uniform lines *if all other things were equal*. But other things are rarely equal. So let me point out the sort of variable factors which influence whether or not secularization will carry over into less-central areas.

*1. Promoted or prohibited?*    One of the leading enemy agents once reported attending a Vatican conference on secularization at which a priest was explaining the process to a Christian Democrat politician.[19] Halfway through his explanation, he was cut short as the politician raised his hand and said firmly, "We will not permit it!" This struck the agent as very funny at the time. Ten years later, however, he watched the Iranian revolution on television and heard the passionate chanting of "Allah akbar!" (God is great!) by the followers of the Ayatollah Khomeini. Suddenly the earlier incident no longer seemed so absurd. Secularization, he realized, might not only be reversed by religious renewal, but also stopped before it starts by prohibition.

This illustrates the first variable affecting distribution. Does the society or culture in question favor modernization, or is it opposed to it (as in Iran)? Where there is a high degree of resistance to modernization, the impact of secularization is likely to be least. Theoretically, this would be most true of societies which are so opposed to modernization that they reject the central carriers altogether (saying no to modern technology as well as modern morality). But such reactionary societies are rare. More common will be those (Saudi Arabia or China, for example) which seek to control the carry-over from the central sectors to the less-central sectors such as family and moral life (saying yes to modern technology, no to modern morality).

Notice the strategic significance of this point. Since modernization can be prohibited to some extent, religion will still be found flourishing in certain parts of the world, in spite of the rise in secularization generally. But this poses no problem to us for several reasons. To begin with, the modern world arose in the so-called Christian countries, so Christianity has already been incurably infected. The strength to control secularization is quite beyond the modern church.

One could speculate whether Christianity would have resisted secularization any better than Islam, if it had the same cultural breathing space which Islam has had. (For those who don't like the fruits of development, to be further behind in modernization is to be better off.) But such speculation would be idle. The modern church does not have the luxury of such a cultural time lag. By definition it could never be far enough behind to consider rejecting modernization altogether.

At any rate, even religion which does manage to resist secularization will not trouble us. This is partly because it will not be Christianity (for the reason above) and partly because it can be encouraged as an alternative to the church. Islam fits in beautifully here. Along with Marxism, it stands as a serious rival to the church. It too takes history seriously and insists that its principles are for the whole of life and not for the private sphere only.

The persistence of religion isn't likely to get out of hand, because resistance as determined as the Ayatollah's is bound to be rare or brief. It's just not pragmatic. Watch the oil-rich Muslims trimming their Islamic principles to suit their enjoyment of "the good life," not to mention their new-found banking and insurance concerns. For obvious reasons, few countries are following the Ayatollah and saying so emphatic a no to the blandishments of modernity. Most are opting for development and by doing so walk into the arms of secularization.

**2. *Close or distant?*** Years ago, when the first surveys were taken in France to see how far secularization had bitten into the minds and habits of French people, I was intrigued to see the patterns which emerged.[20] Men were noticeably more secular in outlook and practice than women, the middle-aged more than the young or the old, those living in cities more than those living in the country, Protestants more than Roman Catholics, and industrial workers more than those in the traditional professions (such as medicine or law) or traditional occupations (such as shopkeeping).

Such findings highlight a second variable. Other things being equal, people tend to be secularized according to how close or distant they are from the primary carriers of modernity. Those most in contact with the carriers are most likely to be infected. Men were more secular than women, for example, because they were (then) more likely than women to be working in the modern sector.

There are exceptions to this variable, one of which is important enough to form the next variable. But most exceptions are quite understandable and serve only to prove the rule. In southern Spain, for instance, religious practice in certain rural areas is much less than in the towns—the opposite of the general rule.[21] But the reason is clear. The church neglects those country areas badly; and those living there are not a typical, rural population but a highly mobile, rootless work force brought in for seasonal jobs, such as grape picking.

**3. *Low vitality or high vitality?*** The obvious exception, which stubbornly refuses to fit the first two categories, is the United States. You will see this when you take up your work there, and unless you can account for it, you will neither do justice to the evidence nor fully appreciate the Council's approach. The anomaly is plain. No Christian country has made a clearer separation of church and state, yet in none is there a closer relationship between religion and society. If modernization automatically produces secularization, why is the United States both the most modern and the most religious of modern countries?[22]

This paradox is explained by a third variable. While all modern countries, including the United States, have been secularized in the sense that their central sectors are secular, the degree to which there is also a carry-over into other spheres depends on the spiritual and social vitality of the faith in that country. By spiritual vitality, I mean just that—a spiritual liveliness which is the regrettable, but rare, sign of the direct work of the Adversary. By social vitality I mean something different—namely, that religion may sometimes gain its strength, not from a purely spiritual source, but from its more social and historical role, such as when it acts as the guardian of cultural identity (as Catholicism does in Poland) or as court chaplain to the political establishment (as in many forms of European nationalism).

Wherever the spiritual and social vitality of a country's faith are both low (as was the case in pre-Revolutionary France), secularization in the central sectors will join hands with secularism and carry over easily into other areas of social life. In cases like these, we can pull out all the stops, go the whole way, and work for the *virtual collapse* of the church. You can see this most starkly in the great wine-producing areas of France, including Champagne, Burgundy, the Garonne and the Midi Coast. Once they were centers of Christian spirituality, but local conditions such as unfavorable land tenure had turned them into seedbeds of discontent. Workers recruited from these regions for the new industries were spiritually indifferent even before they moved to the cities.[23]

But where the spiritual and social vitality of a country's faith is high (as was and is the case in the U.S.), there is some natural immunity to the carriers of secularization. We therefore have to be satisfied for the moment with completing the first of a two-stage movement. Since the vitality of faith temporarily prevents secularization from spreading into other areas, we work on making sure that the central sectors are irreversibly secularized. The vitality of faith is therefore not what it seems, because it is tightly contained. It is still too early to achieve its virtual collapse, but we can succeed in effecting a *vital change*. This is the first step toward eventual collapse.

Unfortunately, the United States is showing signs of a renewal of faith which has both spiritual and social vitality. For us to strike for the collapse of the church is, therefore, out of the question. But once you appreciate the vital change which we have caused, you will see that collapse is only a matter of time. What's good for General Motors may or may not be good for America, but General Motors is secularized, and much of the rest of America will follow.

This third variable helps to explain why the impact of secularization on the United States has been so different from that on Europe. Some field agents have even queried whether we are gaining in the U.S. at all. Their doubts are groundless. Our plans are on schedule. Nothing is out of control. The American situation has simply required a different response. (Later in the briefing I will pick up this question of the distinctive U.S. situation in much greater detail.)

Certainly we have already cooled the spiritual temperature in Europe to an Arctic level where only the hardiest of believers can survive, and then only by huddling together in their spiritual igloos. ("Always winter, never Christmas," as one of their agents laments.) But, as you will soon discover, the steamy, equatorial spiritual heat of the United States has its advantages—not least in allowing us to cultivate exotic, poisonous hybrids which would thrive in no other climate.

This first main pressure, secularization, or the Cheshire-cat factor, is by far the most difficult to understand. But, as you can see, it is also the most basic and devastating. Once its work has been done, the way is open for the other two pressures to operate. Where secularization has occurred, we gain far more than a beachhead on the fringes of the modern world. We have access to its very command center.

# MEMORANDUM
## 4

**SUBJECT:**
# THE PRIVATE-ZOO FACTOR
**FROM:**
DEPUTY DIRECTOR,
CENTRAL SECURITY COUNCIL
**TO:**
DIRECTOR DESIGNATE,
LOS ANGELES BUREAU
**CLASSIFICATION:**
ULTRA SECRET

■

"I believe in the discipline of silence," said George Bernard Shaw about the original Quaker style of worship, "and could talk about it for hours." Shaw's wit fastens here on the sort of contradictions that are basic to human nature. Have you noticed, though, how the number of such human contradictions is increasing dramatically in the modern world?

You can see this supremely in what might be called "sunset values." These are values which modern people prize highly and hold passionately, but which really gain much of their intensity from the fact that they are about to disappear or be changed forever. Like the setting sun, such values make a flamboyant show at the end.

Take, for instance, the contradiction in the mounting concern for wildlife and the wilderness. As the modern world encroaches on more and more of the natural world the only wildlife left will be in zoos. Conservation will then justify captivity. How else, it will be argued, can wild creatures be preserved from the advancing jaws of development?

But the question then is: What will *preserved* mean? How wild is the Bengal tiger in the wildlife park? Or the lone seal bulleting around its circular pond? Or the elephant on its ritual route behind the moat? How wild is wildlife in captivity?

I'll leave you to ponder the ironies, a major preoccupation of yours, it seems. But what I'm getting at is that wild animals, once savage and dangerous to human beings, have become little more than pets; and what has happened to wildlife is nothing compared with the taming of religion.

Look at it from the point of view of the religious believers. Religion to them was once life's central mystery, its worship life's most awesome experience, its faith life's broadest canopy of meaning as well as its deepest guarantee of belonging. Yet today, where religion still survives in the modern world, no matter how passionate or "committed" the individual believer may be, it amounts to little more than a private preference, a spare-time hobby, a leisure pursuit.

The Cheshire-cat factor has paved the way for this, but it's mainly the work of the second great pressure that modernization has brought to bear on religion. This, which in many ways is the reverse side of the Cheshire-cat factor, is the private-zoo factor, so called because it domesticates the hitherto untamable world of the spirit and fences in the once unbounded provinces of the Adversary. Religious variety, color and life still remain. But here, too, the price of conservation is captivity.

Incidentally, I could sense in your response to the last memo your evident distaste for the notion of new gods and old ghosts "squatting" in the post-Christian house. That is your support for a fastidious secularism coming through. Don't forget that from the slave-based Athens of Pericles to the leisured, aristocratic world of the Enlightenment *philosophes,* pure secularist philosophies have always been a minority interest. I agree with you that the "exorcism" of the Christian house may introduce some post-Christian squatters of a rather unsavory sort. But be assured: Such scruffy spirituality will also be in strict captivity. And the Director has plans for it.

The private-zoo factor is a tricky one to work with and requires a rare blend of cool thinking and deft handling. To be candid (and I will be, since these memos are for your eyes only), this is one area where I sometimes feel less than sanguine. Not that I think we've miscalculated. But I do suspect that several of the CSC and many of the Bureau directors underestimate the risks and the skill required to use this pressure.

Can you imagine the hunter relaxing when he has cornered his tiger? He may be seconds away from capturing a prize quarry, but those seconds are the most dangerous of all. We face a similar risk at this stage of the Operation. The risk is that in cornering faith and driving it toward captivity, we may accidentally arouse its ancient energy and vision. Then, in an instinctive last stand, it could elude our capture and break loose again.

Make no mistake. Faith is never more dangerous than when it senses danger. In fighting for life, the conscience, the will, the mind and the emotions of an individual can be fanned into a blaze of pent-up conviction. Christianity grew strong this way in the first place, and periods of revival have always had this same personal element at their heart. So for religion to be personal is for religion to be powerful, but if and only if it does not stop there.

That is our cue. If we can ensure that faith is *personal but no more*, then we can quietly coax it into a corner from which it will never emerge. On the whole, we are managing to do this, and so far the private-zoo factor is working well for us. But, unlike the Cheshire-cat factor, it is not automatic; and, unlike the smorgasbord factor, it is not easy. I would therefore advise you to keep a constant watch on your agents in this Operation. Mistakes are likely to be costly, and they are not likely to be forgiven. Success has a hundred fathers; defeat is an orphan, as the Director allows no one to forget.

## The Heart of the Matter

The technical term for the private-zoo factor is *privatization*. By privatization I mean *the process by which modernization produces a cleavage between the public and the private spheres of life and focuses the private sphere as the special arena for the expansion of individual freedom and fulfillment.*[1]

Naturally, there has always been a distinction between the more personal and the more public areas of life, but until recently the relationship between them was marked by a continuum rather than a cleavage. Today it might as well be the Grand Canyon.

On one side of the cleavage is the public sphere,[2] the macroworld of giant institutions (government departments such as the Treasury, large corporations such as General Motors and IBM, military complexes such as the Pentagon). To many people, this public world is a large and impersonal one, anonymous in its character and incomprehensible in its inner workings. That is not to say that people are necessarily lost or alienated in such a world. They play their roles and earn their incomes there. But by no stretch of the imagination do most people see it as the place where they find their identity and exercise their freedom.

On the other side of the cleavage is the private sphere, the microworld of the family and private associations, the world of personal tastes, sports, hobbies and other leisure pursuits. Very significantly, it is on this side of the divide that the church has made her home.

Two developments have contributed to the special emphasis on the family in this private sphere. First, there has been a crucial *shrinkage* in the way the family previously extended into public life. The family has been reduced to its smallest size (the extended family, such as it was, giving way to the nuclear family), and relieved of many of its former roles, such as in economic production (the cottage industry) or education.

Second, there has been an equally crucial *shift* to an important new role. The private sphere in general, and the family in particular, now have one overriding concern: the personal needs, expectations and fulfillment of the individual. At the same time, the private sphere has become the sphere of spending rather than earning, consumption rather than production. This fateful convergence creates the possibility of "conspicuous consumption"[3]—spending which is not a matter of need but a matter of identity. Material belongings are the social badge of status and success.

All this means that most modern people experience the private sphere as an island where the "real self" lives. Under the impact of the microchip revolution, this feeling can only grow. Home information centers, for example, will dramatically increase the range of activities which people can attempt and achieve without ever leaving the private world of the so-called electronic cottage. It is interesting, isn't it, that the "real self" does not live in the "real world"? You will see just how interesting.

## Negative Side Effects

The three main pressures which modernization is bringing to bear on religion did not originate with us. They work decisively in our favor. But don't ever forget that each of them is double-edged. Here and there they carry disadvantages for us, so we need to assess them carefully before deciding how best to exploit them.

There are two potential disadvantages of the process of privatization. The first is that *it does represent authentic freedom.* Compared with the situation in the past, privatization permits more people to do more, buy more and travel more than ever before. You must add to this the fact that, unlike people in totalitarian societies, privatized Westerners *have* a private world. Big Brother is not watching them, at least not in this part of their lives.

It's easy to caricature the results of this freedom. Often they are chaotic. Do-it-yourself beliefs become as simple as do-it-yourself plumbing. Psyches can be redecorated as quickly as living rooms. People switch convictions as easily as television channels. But let's be sure of this: To most people, the private world (in the words of a pop song) is "a world of our own." It represents extraordinary freedom and the chance to think and act independently. So beware. This is a potential flash point for us, and we shall have to monitor it closely.

The second problem from our perspective is that the *private sphere serves as a form of compensation.* Many people make up for in the private spheres what they're denied in the public sphere. The private sphere works for them like a safety valve or fire escape. "Out there" (in the public sphere) they may wear a uniform, whether factory overalls or a three-piece suit, play a role and be identified by a number. "But here's one place" (in the private sphere), they say, where they can "get out of those things" and be themselves.

In the public sphere, relationships are necessarily partial, superficial and functional, but in the private sphere they can be total, deep, personal and face to face. This can cut various ways. A person who is frustrated by being a small fish in a big pond at work can play the big fish in a small pond at home. Another can find the anonymity of work an escape from the problems of life at home.

The element of compensation has its advantages for us, since it acts as an opiate against public reality. But once more, the problem is that at its heart lies a dangerous core of freedom, independence and choice.

**Known Benefits**
The advantages of privatization for our plans more than outweigh these two disadvantages. As I lay out some of these advantages, you will see why we are able to move in on religion and drive it into captivity. You asked why "10-10-80" couldn't conceivably work the other way 'round, the presently complacent 80 per cent being mobilized by the 10 per cent who are exceptions. What follows provides the answer.

*1. Limited and limiting.*   The first great advantage is that *privatization ultimately acts as a decisive limitation on freedom.* Granted, it offers freedom, unprecedented freedom, but only within strict limits. In the end the price of this freedom is captivity. What do they want to pursue? Yoga? Satan worship? Spouse swapping? Bridge playing? Speaking in tongues? Fellowship groups? Let them feel free. The choice is theirs. Everything is permitted in the private sphere. Money, time and, to a mild extent, local sensitivities, are the only limits.

But what will they discover if they try to bring those personal commitments out into the public sphere? The same Grand Canyon, metaphorically speaking. The world of work—the world of Wall Street, Capitol Hill, Gulf and Western and NASA—is quite a different world and has quite different ways. Personal preferences have no place there. Prayer breakfasts *before* work maybe. For the East-West set, TM in the lunch hour perhaps. It may be called "full-time service" if it is work on the mission field, of course. But in the normal working world, personal convictions, along with hats and coats, are to be left at the door.

Privatization thus spells freedom but only in the private sphere. In fact, far from being the arena of choice and creativity it sets itself up as, the private sphere is really a sort of harmless play area.[4] Individuals are free to build a world of their own to their hearts' content—so long as they rock none of the boats in the real world. For the religious believer, the private sphere serves as a sort of spiritual Indian reservation or Bantustan, a homeland for separate spiritual development set up obligingly by the architects of secular society's apartheid.

Having put it this strongly, let me allow you to bring in any counter-evidence you may wish. Three objections I will grant you. First, that disastrous outbreaks of spiritual revival in history have always featured highly personal faith (you well know of the cell groups set up by Wesley in the eighteenth-century awakening). Second, that there are signs of such an outbreak in the Third World today, especially in places like Costa Rica and Korea or in Chinese provinces like Honan. These are places where the fire is spreading fastest and most uncontrollably when the spiritual movement is rooted in home groups. Third, that the last decade has seen a decided shift in the West toward more personal, informal and home-based expressions of faith.

All this I freely concede. Such evidence only illustrates why this pressure has risks and why we can't be too careful. But remember, our sector of responsibility is the modern sphere alone; citing premodern examples is beside the point. We are not concerned with the past or with the Third World where it is still not modernized. And in the modern world the very point of using privatization is that it adds a new and unexpected catch. It guarantees that personal freedom is no longer what it has been in the past.

There is therefore only one serious issue for us: Is the movement of renewal in the West still contained by the *social inhibitions* which accompany privatization, or is it marked by a *spiritual inspiration* which is breaking out of the bounds of the private sphere? Put the question that way, and you will see your answer. Look closely at the marked shift of emphasis in religion over the last ten years—from institutions to individuals, from programs to people, from the formal to the informal, from the mind to the feelings, from the set-form to the freeform, from the head to the whole body, from the word to the spirit, from the local church to the home.

Would you have taken that as a disturbing sign of authentic revival? In the past the answer would have been yes. But, thanks to privatization, that is no longer so. The outbreak of spiritual concern may be authentic, but the boa-like squeeze of privatization acts to constrict and smother any dynamic that could have culture-wide significance.

Put simply, the charismatic renewal generally and your American renewal in particular are not what they seem to be nor what they wish they were. Their weakness is not that renewal starts in the private world, but that *it ends there too*. Spiritual inspiration they may have. But social inhibitions overwhelm them in the end.

If this were not so, the renewal movement would be extremely dangerous. It has reawakened a hunger for transcendence which refuses to be satisfied with secularism. It has rediscovered how to exercise a diversity of individual gifts which threaten to by-pass professional categories. It stresses the practice of community and claims to answer the modern cry for meaning and belonging. Were it not for the grip of privatization (and of a further tactic I will introduce later), all this could become disastrous.

We've come a very long way in a hundred fifty years. Lord Melbourne, British prime minister in the 1830s, once listened to a pointed sermon and made the indignant remark: "Things have come to a pretty pass when religion is allowed to invade the private life!" He was a perceptive fellow. Personal faith was seen as very demanding. In touching the personal life, it threatened to become a force that reached out into all of life and left nothing untouched. That, for a prime minister in the days of the British Empire, was a bit much.

Compare that with the present view of personal faith. Recently a historian commented on what he had observed of the Christian faith in America: "Socially irrelevant, even if privately engaging."[5] We could ask for no better. Lord Melbourne would be untroubled now. In today's world things have come to a pretty pass if religion is allowed to invade the *public* life.

In terms of Christian theory, privatization means that the grand, global umbrella of faith has shrunk to the size of a plastic rain hat. Total life norms have become part-time values. In terms of Christian practice, watch your average Christian business person or politician. Are there family prayers at home before leaving for work? The private sphere. Are there Bible studies with colleagues at the office? Still the private sphere.

Look for a place where the Christian's faith makes a difference at work beyond the realm of purely personal things (such as witnessing to colleagues and praying for them, or *not* swearing and *not* fiddling with income tax returns). Look for a place where the Christian is thinking "Christianly" and critically about the substance of work (about, say, the use of profits and not just personnel; about the ethics of a multinational corporation and not just those of a small family business; about a just economic order and not just the doctrine of justification). You will look for a very long time. He or she may be "into religion," but so are colleagues "into golfing" or "into theater" or a score of other hobbies.

A Christian's priorities outside the office may be God, family and business, but once inside the office that order is reversed. Such Christians are of little use to the Adversary and pose no threat to us. The fascinating thing is that their deficiency is so minor. It's not that they aren't where they should be, but that *they aren't what they should be where they are.*

Do you see what an opening this is? We can encourage Christians to accept as normal a damaging degree of spiritual specialization. When this happened before, in the fourth century, the gap was between the "advanced" believer who was truly spiritual and the "average" believer who muddled along as best he could with a less demanding rule of life. It was this widening gulf which brought the conversion of the Roman world to a halt.[6] The new gulf is different —between the private and the public, rather than the average and the advanced—but our goal is the same: to create such a spiritual specialization that Christian penetration of the modern world comes to a grinding halt.

Let these four words *privately engaging, socially irrelevant* be engraved on your mind. That's what privatization has done to renewal in the modern world. "Jesus is Lord," they may declare (and sing and strum on their guitars to their hearts' content). But what do they demonstrate? Little better than a spare-time faith and a pocket-discipleship. The once wild animal may roar, but safely behind bars.

**2. *Fragmenting and dislocating.*** I've spent time on the first advantage of privatization, since it is absolutely critical to us, but let me cover briefly some further advantages. A second one is that *privatization induces a sense of fragmentation or dislocation.* In the highly complex and diversified conditions of the modern world, there is not only greater freedom *within* each separate sphere, there is a greater difference (and distance) *between* each.

This means, on the one hand, that people today are anonymous to more people and in more situations than ever before. Just to get to their daily destinations, they must cross life as they cross a crowded concourse in an airport terminal. On the other hand, the different worlds that are their destination are *very* different. Worlds which are only minutes apart physically may be light years apart morally or spiritually. A person's life can therefore come to resemble a nonstop process of commuting between almost completely separate, even segregated, worlds.

We must see that the net effect of these constant crossings is spiritual compartmentalism, if not ethical and psychological confusion. For some people, moving in different worlds and having to wear different hats are a source of only minor irritation. Others can be driven into a state of deep inner division, as Karl Mannheim remarked of the bureaucrat: "He lives in two worlds, and he must therefore, so to speak, have two souls."[7]

The potential here for spiritual, moral and intellectual schizophrenia is great. Christians have always been warned against the hypocrisy of double-thinking. But now that they're juggling with double, triple and quadruple-living, modular morality and compartmentalized convictions are becoming as interchangeable as *lego*-like lifestyles.

At the very least, this fragmentation fosters the breathless, strung-out feeling characteristic of busy modern Christians. Better still, it means that modern Christians are denied the chance of a total expression of their gifts and personalities. Best of all, it makes certain that there is no Christian mind integrating all of life, only a personal faith with compartments between its various disciplines and activities. (One mind for church, another for the classroom; one for reading the Bible, another for reading the newspaper; one for the world of the family, another for the world of business.) In the busy rush of life's commuting, Christian convictions are boxed-in as neatly and firmly as the commuter behind his paper in a crowded morning train.

*3. Unstable and unrealistic.* A third advantage to us is that *privatization creates an inherently unstable private sphere.* Consider the difference between steering a sail board and piloting an ocean liner like the QE2. For anyone wanting the freedom to follow every caprice of the breeze, wind surfing is the obvious choice. For crossing the Atlantic, however, the QE2 is a surer bet.

From the perspective of the believer in the private sphere, much of the institutional church—sometimes at the local level, certainly at the denominational level—appears about as maneuverable and responsive as an ocean liner. So the growing desire is to cut loose and find the freedom and exhilaration of spiritual wind surfing in the burgeoning home groups.

We should not try to discourage this idea. These groups are not only as free as a sail board, but as collapsible too. There are two reasons for this instability. On the one hand, the private sphere is decidedly *understructured*.[8] The extended family (such as it was) has shrunk into the nuclear family, and religion has retreated from its previous position of influence in the public sphere. Thus the two strongest supports which traditionally undergirded people's private lives and tied them into a wider public world have been sabotaged in a stroke.

The result is a crisis in the traditional ways of setting up and running the private life, a crisis which leaves people more uncertain as well as more free. Conventional values are no longer taken for granted, and the traditional supporting web of family, friends, neighbors and colleagues can no longer be counted on without question. Family members may be scattered across the world, and neighbors and colleagues change with the speed of a game of musical chairs. Some sort of supporting web can certainly be rewoven and maintained, but only by a conscious effort of will. Privatized man is free to be Atlas to his own world, although a somewhat anxious Atlas to a largely do-it-yourself world.

On the other hand, the private sphere is distinctly *oversold*.[9] It has become the sphere of spending rather than earning, and of personal fulfillment rather than public obligation. Naturally then, when conspicuous consumption grafts spending into identity and fulfillment, appetites become insatiable and expectations unrealistic. In short, privatized man is not only an anxious Atlas, but a spoilt Narcissus. He wants more, and he wants it now. After all, to others at least, he is what he consumes. And so is she.

This combination (institutionally understructured, ideologically oversold) is a potent blend which makes the private sphere highly unstable and volatile. One moment the impression is all freedom. Do-it-yourself this, do-it-yourself that, and almost miraculously little worlds arise overnight, replete with new homes, new friends, new lifestyles, new identities. The next moment, the impression is all fragility. The neighborhood changes, separation and divorce are in the air, children drop out, sickness strikes, a job is axed and in an instant liberty becomes anxiety becomes catastrophe. For every newly constructed miniworld, another is collapsing.

Privatized freedom, in other words, is highly precarious. Under-structured, it is the victim of outside forces pulling it apart. Over-sold, it is the victim of inner forces tearing it down. What begins with Atlas ends with Humpty Dumpty, and all the king's counselors, therapists and attorneys can't put the pieces together again.

Both aspects of this general dilemma apply to the religious world too. How privatized faith becomes understructured is evident in many of the fringe groups in the charismatic movement—the "off-off-Broadway" of the world of ecstasy. They cut themselves off from the church of the past and from the wider church around the world, and very often from the local church. In place of these, they concentrate on the private and personal, often in a form no larger than the nuclear family or a home fellowship group. Wind surfing requires a somewhat smaller crew.

Where does this lead? Such groups have a social base which is smaller, shakier and shorter-lived. They lack theology, they lack a sense of history and tradition, they lack discipline and accountabil-ity, and they lack clear boundaries as to what membership involves. Easier to join, they are easier to leave. Launched more easily, they capsize more easily. Viewed overnight, they seem to offer the libera-tion and flexibility of a highly personal, deeply spiritual faith. Viewed over the course of ten years, they have all the ocean-going stability of a cockleshell.

The way in which privatized faith is oversold is equally plain. Drop into your local secular bookstore sometime and size up the amazing range of how-to and can-do publishing. Do people want to improve their memory, banish boredom, relax, cope with stress, overcome fears, brighten their love life? It's all there for them, with self-awareness the dominant theme, and success, wealth and peace of mind close behind. Then visit a local Christian bookstore. The themes and style are precisely the same, only the gloss is different.

Somehow privatization seems to bring out the best in copycat Christianity. Originally it was the words of pop songs which were mimicked. Then the copying craze spread to advertizing jingles ("Jesus is the real thing," brought to you by association with Coca-Cola). Now the instant imitation is the predictable response to every fad. When dieting became fashionable, for example, Propaganda and Disinformation were ready with a line of counterfeit slogans. But they were redundant even before they were released. The Christian ones were far more fatuous. Dieting Christian-style became "Trim for Him." Then, with the stress shifting to fitness, there came *Aerobic Praise, Devotion in Motion, Praise-R-Cise,* and the most astounding so far: the album *Firm Believer* and the slimming slogan, "He must increase but I must decrease."[10] Even P and D were taken aback at first. These slogans were nearly blasphemous by traditional standards. Some other dirty tricksters must be at work. But the slogans proved authentic. Normally, canny copywriters use puns ("Datsun saves") to give their products a leg up, caring little for the original meanings. Incredible as it may seem, Christians do the reverse: They use double meanings to sell their product and not only devalue the original meanings but demean themselves in the process.

*Firm Believer* says it all. With spiritual narcissism so well advanced, "firm believer" is a matter of aerobics rather than apologetics, of human fitness rather than divine faithfulness. Shapeliness is now next to godliness, and to judge by the new "shape-up centers" in Christian stores, training righteous character has given way to trimming the right curves.

Poor old Paul. Wrong again. Bodily exercise now profiteth much —for the record companies at least. Poor old John the Baptist. Decreasing, for him, meant losing his head, not shedding some pounds. But then our bandwagon believers are in danger of losing their heads as well. No wonder such privatized faith has been described as "credit card religion."[11] It takes the waiting out of wanting. It even takes the waiting out of waiting on God.

**4. *Vulnerable and manipulated.*** Each of these previous advantages depends on the gap between the ostensible freedom of the private sphere and the true situation (between the commercial and the catch, as it were). That is equally true of the fourth advantage of privatization—*its unique vulnerability to manipulation.*

Experts in the field diverge here.[12] Some point to the extreme conditioning of the private sphere by forces outside it. As these people see it, in the private sphere of their lives people are little better than cheerful robots, massaged and manipulated by external forces such as advertising and the mass media. Leisure and recreation are as much a serious business (and as much big business) as work. Like their groceries, people's lifestyles and dreams come prepackaged. Others see the impact of privatization as less extreme, simply the carry-over from the public to the private sphere, rather than an extreme conditioning. Either way, the private sphere is undeniably manipulable, and therein lies our chance.

All sorts of manipulations are possible. The privatized person is the "quiet life voter," vulnerable to political propaganda and appeals such as the law-and-order issue on one side or (less obviously) the peace movement on the other. If the ultimate value is survival and the immediate value is personal peace and prosperity, then those brought up to live for themselves will be less inclined to live (or die) for others. Thus talk of law and order, instead of fortifying justice, justifies force and turns a blind eye to its spilling over into violence. Likewise, protest for peace, instead of bringing peace, can become the path to appeasement and so encourage evil and increase the chance of war. The privatized values act like a hidden bias in each case, allowing us to pull off course what Christians recognize as important concerns.

But the privatized person is also a "champion consumer," the target of commercial advertising; a "classic narcissist," client to the multiplying therapeutic agencies in a world in which, as Orwell said, "Freud and Machiavelli have reached the outer suburbs";[13] and a "potential convert" (when not only help but a home is wanted, there is always a cult). The extremes here do not have to be coaxed into a cage; they virtually sit mewing for one.

Notice again how the contradiction between the ostensible freedom and the true situation is entirely to our advantage. Once more privatized freedom is not the freedom it seems. It is what intelligence people might call the "ultimate honey-trap," a snare from which faith cannot even sense that it ought to escape. In the past we have cultivated religious individualism and have found that certain strains of faith such as pietism are particularly fruitful for our purposes. But never have we had such harvest as this. You know that the Greeks defined the idiot as a wholly private person. Privatization multiplies the number of Christians who fall prey to this and makes such idiocy a spiritual condition.

I would not deny that there are exceptions to all this. There are theological traditions (such as the Reformed) which refuse to fall for narrow pietism; or local churches (in the U.S. particularly among the Blacks) which run a variety of community services which are far from privatized and put government welfare to shame; or recent movements which have made a noise about faith in public (though mostly about more personal things, such as abortion and pornography). But these, fortunately, are exceptions. As I told you, "Remember 10-10-80" is the Director's maxim. We are well within our limits as regards the "10" who are exceptions, and nothing rivals privatization in ensuring that we have the "80."

### Set but Not Sprung

We are now at the stage between the setting and the springing of the trap. This is our operational moment of truth when there is no way out but forward. There remains the one major risk to which I have referred. Instead of sealing faith's captivity in the private sphere, something might trigger the reawakening of a faith which is both personal and culturally powerful at once. Faith would then elude capture and break out into the larger world again.

This is unthinkable. Yet I would urge constant vigilance on your field agents at this point. And remind them that privatization is a double-edged sword. Let me conclude with the twin possibilities that constantly face us. The one example serves as an encouragement, the other a warning.

*1. The clergy catch.*   Privatization has an extra twist for ministers. They misinterpret it as a showdown between individualism and institutionalism. Then, seeing themselves as guardians of the institutional church, they stand against the dangers of individualism by bolstering the institution. When this is done (often most successfully), they consider they have saved the day. The institutional church is stronger; individualism and what they think are the only problems of privatization have been overcome.

Do you see the fallacy? The real issue in privatization is not the individual versus the institution, but the private sphere versus the public sphere. So let them, indeed encourage them, to build the biggest, richest, best-known and most successful local churches they like. They will still be in the weekend, week-night world of the private sphere. In point of fact, the greater the empire building of the local church, the deeper the effects of privatization. At a certain point, *every meeting added, every penny collected, means less time and fewer resources for penetrating the public world.* Vested interests in the professional ministry not only prevent ministers from seeing this but intensify the problem.

This elementary ministerial mistake aggravates an ancient handicap which Christians never seem to overcome. By using the word *church* not only of themselves but of their institutions and buildings, Christians create a language which favors the institutional separateness of religion. After all, if this is "the church," everything else must be "the world." There in the so-called edifice complex is the premodern seed of the problem; privatization is only a fertile new soil in which it has flourished.

*2. The Eastern European exception.*   On the other hand, and this is where the situation comes closest to your objection, the church in Eastern Europe stands as a sober warning of what happens when privatization is allowed to become constructive for Christians rather than constricting. There is always a potentially dangerous link between religious conscience and freedom of choice. This means that, in certain (fortunately rare) circumstances, the religion of the heart can become a recess which neither state nor society nor tribe can penetrate. ("Here I stand. I can do no other. So help me God.") It then becomes a citadel of conscience, an altar to a loyalty which supplants loyalty to Caesar.

This sort of thing is far more pernicious than political activism. Look at the early Christians. Christianity, which began as a spiritual commitment practiced in secret, became dominant over more and more of life, eventually undercutting Roman rule and becoming the new principle of public order.

That has not happened in the Western world. Quite the reverse. What once turned the world upside-down has now turned in on itself. But I regret to say that a powerful Christian presence is not out of the question in Eastern Europe. In my judgment our East European Directorate is making a terrible blunder. They could learn something from the old, uncouth schoolboy joke about Christians being like runner beans, never better than when tied to a stake. Abandoning the strategy of subversion through modernization, they have openly and crudely applied ideological pressure to the church.

But what have they achieved? Elements of the faith which were becoming vague and uncertain (and therefore useful to us) have been burnt away under the heat of pressure, and a tough core is emerging, irreducible and quite beyond our reach. Personal faith with a social edge is building up again. Out of the Utopia and into the Gulag was part of the blueprint; out of the Gulag and into the gospel was not.

Have you come across the word *huddle* as American football players use it? Nothing could be further from such all-American machismo than the slightly insecure coziness which the word *huddle* implies in Britain. Personal faith in Eastern Europe is as different as that from the "holy huddle" of faith in the West. Privatized by law as part of the totalitarian repression, it refuses to be personal only, and in the act of resisting confinement it is threatening to become the focus of real power. Not only is it a main channel of dissent, it is also the carrier of cultural identity. The Soviety Union itself could soon be seething with frustrated faith. If the Directorate's stupidities are unchecked, a spiritual and social revolution could become imaginable.[14]

Never forget Eastern European faith. Propaganda and Disinformation can always portray it as the product of ignorant and persecuted peoples, but it's a double warning: first, that personal faith can work against as well as for us; second, that despite initial appearances, cultural seduction is far more effective than blasting away with the blunderbuss of hostile ideology. The race is not to the swift, to borrow a phrase.

Never mistake caution for hesitation. Nothing is insecure but thinking makes it so. Apart from that one tripwire I have indicated, nothing stands between our plans and their consummation. The Director calculates that if we reach the late 1990s without alerting the Western church to the depth of its privatization, victory will be ours soon after the turn of the century. The trap is set. We have about ten years to spring it.

# MEMORANDUM
# 5

**SUBJECT:**
## THE SMORGASBORD FACTOR
**FROM:**
DEPUTY DIRECTOR,
CENTRAL SECURITY COUNCIL
**TO:**
DIRECTOR DESIGNATE,
LOS ANGELES BUREAU
**CLASSIFICATION:**
ULTRA SECRET

■

"Nobody ever went broke underestimating the taste of the American people." H. L. Mencken might repeat his rather wicked remark about some of the "fast food" you will no doubt encounter in Los Angeles. For you, perhaps, it may not be so telling since your immediate contrast will be with the English equivalent. But I never think of his remark without recalling my time in Paris. Mercifully, French democracy did not extend to a popular leveling of taste. They know how to prepare food superlatively, and they know how to serve it.

Have you ever noticed how the way food is served affects the person dining? I remember a curious example of this which I always associate with Los Angeles. I visited your predecessor some years ago just as Sunday brunches were becoming the rage, and he took me to the opening brunch at a lavish, ocean-front hotel.

The opulence and bounty of the table were magnificent, and the endless choice of dishes strained the term *smorgasbord* to the limits. But what was fascinating were people's responses as they faced such an array. A few ate what I suppose they would have ordered anywhere, taking their pick without a moment's hesitation, almost as if the sumptuous range weren't there.

These were the minority. Most acted quite differently. Some treated the choice as a challenge to their capacity, an affront to their reputations for never passing up a bargain. Others were less sure of themselves. They wanted to miss nothing that was tasty or new, and probably no meal in all their lives was chosen and eaten so self-consciously. They inspected the full board, weighed the options, asked advice of those ahead, and dithered forever before finally selecting some food. Clearly, the surfeit of choice threatened to play havoc not only with their figures, but with their peace of mind.

That is a trivial incident (hardly the sort that would figure in your reports to the CSC), but it captures the essence of the third pressure we are bringing to bear on the church. It was in fact this incident which gave the third pressure its code name—the smorgasbord factor.

Before I go further, a word about your reports on the advance trips to L.A. In terms of theoretical understanding, you've clearly accomplished the switch from counter-apologetics to cultural subversion as swiftly as I expected. But you hardly seem able to disguise your disdain for the post-secular alternatives to Christianity you've seen in California.

I trust this is only a mild form of culture shock. We hardly expect you to "go native" with some of the target movements, but California is as much the womb of the gods as the dream factory of the Western world. Too great a sense of distaste will be a handicap to you. I'd hate to conclude that your present life is that much of an ivory tower existence.

## The Heart of the Matter

The technical term for the smorgasbord factor is *pluralization,* a dry term for a devastating process. By pluralization I mean *the process by which the number of options in the private sphere of modern society rapidly multiplies at all levels, especially at the level of world views, faiths and ideologies.*[1] The key feature here is not just variety but such extreme variety within a single society.

This (unlike secularization) is neither radically new nor difficult to understand. The first century A.D. was a period marked by a similar pluralism. The collapse of confidence in the classical gods of Greece and Rome had left a cavernous vacuum, and into it flowed every imaginable kind of popular philosophy, esoteric cult and mystery religion (including, alas, the Adversary's).

You might think that this early experience of pluralism would have prepared Christians for resisting pluralization today. Quite the contrary. Whereas once pluralism left them more sure, it now leaves them less sure, and their moral and intellectual caving in resembles the notorious "failure of nerve" which characterized the popular mood of the first century when the classical religions failed. There are simple reasons for this. The subsequent experience of being virtually a monopoly has disarmed Christians and made them forget what the challenge of pluralism was like. Also, the modern brand of pluralization they have unleashed on themselves is a uniquely powerful one. And this time it has come hand in hand with secularization. The result has been quite sensational.

Pluralization is therefore by no means new. But it does run counter to more normal human experience which is characterized by a desire for the underlying unity of things. Every society has had differences within it, such as differences of work, rank or tradition. But at the same time there has usually been underlying cohesion, and often the most cohesive force in any community has been religion.

In Europe, for instance, despite the enormous diversity (such as the differences of language and the presence of Jews, Muslims and atheists), the underlying cohesion was provided by Christianity.

That's why the traditional role of religion has been described as a "sacred canopy"[2] or "global umbrella."[3] It overarched all of society and culture, defining the world and determining the ways of those who lived under its shelter. What it denied was forbidden; what it ignored did not exist.

Do you see the measure of our success? Today, pluralization sees to it that there is no sacred canopy, only millions of small tents; no global umbrella, only a bewildering range of pocket umbrellas for those who care to have one. The grand overseer has been reduced to being one of a jostling crowd of job seekers and volunteers. The once-commanding symbol of unity has become just one more element in the abstract mosaic of diversity.

### Roads to the Present Position

*1. The Christian contribution.*    A revealing way for you to trace the rise of pluralization is to study its peculiarly Christian origins. By its very character, the pluralizing potential is inherent in Christianity itself.[4] "In the world, but not of it," Christianity stands as a permanent criticism of every given, every established institution, every rival belief. By calling for a transference of allegiance ("repentance and faith"), it unmistakably draws a line and calls for choice. Thus the Christian gospel always insists on an alternative perspective and as such is a generator of choices and dissent. This, as we've seen in the past, is the source of its socially disruptive power.

But what was inherent in Christianity became rampant after the Protestant Reformation and began to work back on itself. Protestants rejected papal authority and unwittingly began the fateful swing to the authority of personal conscience, which was soon indistinguishable from a riot of personal choice and individualism.

Strictly speaking, the Reformation did not introduce pluralism nor did it intend to. Indeed, Protestants at first tried to defend their separate monopolies as zealously as Catholics had defended the whole before. But in the wake of the wars of religion, the irrepressible urge toward pluralization was born, and we have fostered it carefully ever since. Christians may point to their more virtuous contributions (the generating of choices, the respect for conscience), but the contribution of their vices was as important. Pluralization gathered momentum through the fragmentation of Christendom and through the tolerance bred by widespread disillusionment with Christian fanaticism and bigotry.

You move much closer to the present with the invention of the denomination (as with so many things, "made in the U.S.A."). Prior to the American experience, a national church had territorial claims and its membership was virtually established by birth. But those who came to America were not just from nonconformist groups such as the Baptists, who had rejected national churches; they were also drawn from various state churches, each of which had now lost its territorial supremacy and had arrived to find other former state churches already there.

The result was the modern denomination, the "ex-Church," which has been forced to bow to the permanent presence and competition of other churches within its territory. For a while, the Roman Catholic church, as Lenny Bruce once quipped, was "the only The Church left," but now it is falling nicely in line with the others.

You will appreciate that this kind of pluralization bites far more deeply than denominational differences. It eats into basic beliefs too. What fair-minded modern Christian would argue against the place of the modern denomination? But then, how much can the same Christian still believe that his own denomination has the inside lane on interpretation, especially when he realizes there are some 20,000 others (2,051 in the U.S. alone)?[5] But what then of the absolute truth of his own religion when there are so many other religions? Could that be a historical accident too? Before long the acid of doubt has eaten through to the core.

**2. *The modern addition.*** A second way you might trace the rise of pluralization is to see those forces within modernization which have accelerated the tidal wave of choice and change.[6] These are so obvious they hardly need elaboration. Through the crowding growth of cities, modern people are all much closer, yet stranger, to each

other. Through the explosion of knowledge, other people, other
places, other periods and other psyches are accessible as never before. Through modern travel people can go to any part of the world.
Through modern media the world and all its options can be brought
to them. And so on.

Pluralization is accelerated and intensified in a hundred such
ways. The heightened awareness of the presence of others leads
automatically to a sense of the possibilities for ourselves. In essence,
therefore, modern people scan the smorgasbord and say: *Their*
cuisines, *their* customs, *their* convictions all become *our* choices, *our*
options, *our* possibilities. The widest range of choice is often at the
most trivial levels, but the proliferation of choice at many important levels is staggering.

Life is now a smorgasbord with an endless array of options.
Whether a hobby, vacation, lifestyle, world view or religion, there's
something for everybody—and every taste, age, sex, class and interest. The church of your choice? A liturgy to your liking? (1662?
Series A?) *The Good Food Guide* has its counterpart in *The Good Church
Guide.* Pass down the line; take your pick; mix your own; do your
thing.

We have reached the stage in pluralization where choice is not
just a state of affairs, it is a state of mind. Choice has become a value
in itself, even a priority. To be modern is to be addicted to choice
and change. Change becomes the very essence of life.

**Driving Home the Consequences**
The processes of pluralization are fascinating and the possibilities
they open up kaleidoscopic. But don't miss the wood for the trees.
Our true concern is only with consequences.

What happens when choice becomes a state of mind? Obligation
melts into option, givenness into choice, form into freedom. Facts
of life dissolve into fashions of the moment. But the consequence
we care about most is this: *The increase in choice and change leads to a
decrease in commitment and continuity.*

Imagine someone who owned a silk handkerchief inherited from

his Victorian great-grandfather. If he lost it, he'd search for it every-where. It would be a prized possession, beautiful, old and with special associations. He's "attached to it," he might say. Yet no one in his right mind would become attached to a Kleenex tissue, and it would be absurd to waste time looking for one if it were lost. After all, it's disposable. It's made to be thrown away. Commitment and continuity are entirely foreign to the notion of a paper handker-chief.

Another trivial illustration, you may say. Deliberately so, for the truth about the modern world can be learned as readily from the trivia of life as from the philosopher's essay. Most modern people have a relationship to their choices that's closer to the model of the Kleenex tissue than to that of the silk handkerchief.

There's no nostalgia in that judgment, I assure you. I hold no brief for silk handkerchiefs and no grudge against disposable ones. We are interested in the extension of this mentality to more important areas. What may be trifling at the level of things becomes telling at the level of relationships, societies and above all faiths. What happens when modern people "run through" homes like disposable handkerchiefs? Better still, when they "run through" marriages? Above all, when they "run through" beliefs?

*1. New partners for new phases.*    Look at the question of marriage. Pluralization at the level of relationships is putting a unique strain on Christian marriage, which as it disintegrates puts an added strain on the plausibility of faith and the stability of the church. Christians often forget that the centuries-long persistence of traditional marriage was not due solely to their own principles. True, for a couple to commit themselves to each other "till death us do part" was a matter of principle. But social pressures played their part too.

Traditional communities, mostly rural, were comparatively small and stable. Under such conditions, permissiveness would have led to social chaos. Christian principles were therefore silently supported by strong social pressures. And because people did not live so long in the past, "till death us do part" used to be a realistic assessment of the odds. Today it is more often wishful thinking.

Pluralization has been key in effecting this change. The modern individual lives longer and meets and knows more people than ever before, but is also anonymous in more situations. The average modern Londoner, it is said, meets as many people in one week as a medieval person would have met in a lifetime. His or her lifestyle is accordingly faster, freer and more flexible, just as the average relationship is briefer, more superficial and more functional.

The result? Cultural pressure and Christian principle have dramatically parted company and now work against each other. "Ring the changes!" says the one, "New phases in life. New partners in life!"

"No!" says the other, "If marriage collapses, civilization does too!" Which of the two is winning its case in wider society is easy to see. "It is ridiculous," says Clare Booth Luce, "to think that you can spend your entire life with just one person. Three is about the right number. Yes, I imagine three husbands would do it."[7]

The fashionable philosophy behind this is at its height. With the value of choice and change up and the value of commitment and continuity down, freedom, flexibility and convenience are everything. Lifetime faithfulness has given way to free sex just as formal dining has given way to fast food. Of course, don't expect most people to swing to the silly extremes which magazines extol and moralists attack. Free sex all the time is presumably no more tolerable than fast food all the time.

The damage to Christian faithfulness is done at a far less advanced stage. "Creative divorce" is a little avant-garde for the average Christian, except where you are going. But once change is considered appropriate and necessary and marriage has been boiled down to one thing (the make-or-break achievement of emotional intimacy), faithfulness can easily be made to look constricting and hopelessly old-fashioned ("the sure recipe for a loveless marriage").

It's instructive to examine the range of rationales for change. Some are quite straightforward. Their partners no longer "fulfill" them, and they want to get out. But keep your eyes open for more sophisticated cases, particularly those infected by a rationale which is the product of privatization and pluralization combined.

For instance, a Christian conservative writes that the break-up of his marriage was a sad but "healthy new beginning for each of us in our own way."[8] And he continues that he was called by faith like Abraham to leave the security of marriage to embark on a spiritual pilgrimage toward emotional authenticity.

Another writes, "I hope my wife will never divorce me, because I love her with all my heart. But if one day she feels I am minimizing her or making her feel inferior or in any way standing in the light that she needs to become a person God meant her to be, I hope she'll be free to throw me out even if she's one hundred. There is something more important than our staying married, and it has to do with integrity, personhood, and purpose."[9]

The ultimate in refinement are the disingenuous ones who claim to be *separating out of faithfulness to Christ!* Once this would have meant a Christian husband or wife left by the non-Christian partner because of the faith itself. Now it often means a Christian divorcing another Christian over a Christian issue.

Would you have thought, for example, that a commitment to a simple lifestyle could ever lead to divorce? Yes, one writer urges today, "The split finally comes when one recognizes that this kind of conscience can't be compromised. There are levels of importance and urgency in biblical morality. And Jesus' driving concern for the coming of the Kingdom, as a counter to the culture, far outweighed his concern for the maintenance of family structures. There can be as much sin involved in trying to perpetuate a dead or meaningless relationship as in accepting the brokenness, offering it to God, and going on from there."[10] Disobeying Christ out of faithfulness to Christ! The irony is exquisite.

So far, ordinary believers have been slow to succumb to these trends, but the recent epidemic of divorce among clergy and Christian celebrities is the breakthrough for which we've worked. Divorce is now in the very air they breathe. The opinion-formers are going down, and the sheep are bound to follow. "A fish decays from its head first," they say in the intelligence world. Or, as the Director puts it more pertinently, a Christian celebrity sneezes and the church catches the cold.

**2. *Will the center hold?*** Western democracy is another important area where the strains of pluralization can be clearly seen. Recent political discussion in America, for example, amounts to moral civil war over issues like abortion. This is significant. So long as there was a widespread moral consensus in society, Americans were remarkably successful in tolerating extreme religious diversity. But this is no longer the case. Advanced pluralization threatens the stability of Western democracies by calling into question the values undergirding their national legitimacy and unity. Soon they will have little more holding them together than a fragile web of technology through such things as communication satellites, computers and traffic lights. The real U.S. motto might already be: "In electronic surveillance we trust."

This sort of problem will soon raise some fundamental questions for Western democracies. With no ethical north star, there is a navigational crisis of leadership. One of the most challenging questions can be put like this: Can Western liberalism survive the logic of its own increasing pluralism and fragmentation in order to be strong enough to resist totalitarianism and yet remain true to its promise of individual freedom?

If we play this carefully according to the Director's plan, we can drive the church between a rock and a hard place. Insofar as pluralization succeeds, Christianity will become just one option among many; insofar as some future monopoly succeeds, either Christianity will be excluded from the monopoly altogether, or it will be included on terms which in the end will empty it of any content. Our prospects are excellent either way. The Director's lead has proved unerring.

## Commitment-Shy Convictions

When all is said and done, only one level of pluralization really concerns us—the pluralization of beliefs and believing. Commitment-shy faith is a contradiction in terms, you might think, but we've achieved it in various unnoticed ways. Think of some of the side effects which pluralization has had on faith.

One is that *pluralization creates in the modern believer a high degree of self-consciousness.*[11] Each choice raises questions. Might they? Could they? Should they? Will they? Won't they? What if they had? What if they hadn't? And so on. The forest of choices raised by modern options leads deeper and deeper into the dark freedom, then the even darker anxiety, of seemingly infinite possibility.

Like a hall of mirrors, the reflections recede forever. Choice is no longer simple. Choosing is never complete. The outside world becomes more questionable, the inside world more complex. What can they believe? What ought they to do? Who are they? Modern people are constant question marks to each other. Permanent self-consciousness is the price of modern choice.

"He who never visits," runs an old African saying, "thinks his mother is the only cook." Today's believer hasn't the excuse of such blissful ignorance, and with the wider outlook comes not only self-consciousness but uncertainty . . . anxiety . . . doubt. We don't need to force this. Pluralization is an acid that works slowly but efficiently. Modern faith is rarely as assured as it sounds, and the few remaining pockets of certainty can be driven toward defensiveness and fanaticism.

A second, related side effect is that *because of pluralization modern believers have become conversion-prone.*[12] Just as the bedrock of faith was traditionally solid and reassuring, so the turn-around of conversion was traditionally complete and lasting. Reorientation to a new life, new world, new relationships, was radical, but Christians did not see this as unreasonable: It was a once-in-a-lifetime requirement that was expected to last forever.

This too has changed. Faith's precariousness leaves it prone to being converted—and reconverted—and reconverted. Or, as we have recently perfected it in American Christian circles, "Born again and again and again . . . " *ad infinitum.* In today's pluralized, mobile society, the once-telling testimony is reduced to the status of a spiritual visiting card, one that often needs a change of address.

Multiple conversions are now common, but the special conditions of periods like the 1960s step the pace up even further. Jerry Rubin, for instance, a master of spiritual switchcraft, claimed to have experienced eighteen different "trips" in five years, ranging from EST to bioenergenetics.[13] Not that these fruitless exploits have much value to us in themselves. What matters is their general aftertaste.

Slowly a whole generation grows shy of commitment, embarrassed by conviction. For the counter-cultural type, the order of the day was "hang loose"; today's version is "laid back." For the religious liberal, the passwords are "ambiguity" (never certainty) and "reflection" (never revelation). The general result is the same. The search itself is the only truth. To be on the pilgrimage is the only progress. All else is yesterday's arrogance, passing out of the reach or the desire of today's thoughtful person.

A third side effect of pluralization is also to our advantage. *Pluralization reduces the necessity of choosing at all.*[14] In other words, the extension of choice leads to the evasion of choice.

Christians work best in an either/or situation. Let them put the choice starkly, and even the air will be charged with the responsibility of decision. The choice matters. The choice must be made. The choice cannot be ducked. Choose. But having too many choices leads either to a sense of vertigo or to a yawn.

Back in 1885 Pope Leo XII barked out the warning, "The equal toleration of all religions . . . is the same thing as atheism."[15] Dead right, of course, but a trifle indelicate in the modern ecumenical climate. We can expect such archaic sentiments to be ignored. Far more likely is the continuing trend toward a multiplication of choices in which would-be competitors cancel each other out, leading toward the neutralization of values in particular and intellectual chaos in general.

The net effect of all this is that pluralization acts on Christian faith as a sort of nonstick coating. Christians and convictions were once inseparable. Pluralization, though, acts like a spiritual Teflon, sealing Christian truth with a slippery surface to which commitment will not adhere. The result is a general increase in shallowness, transience and heresy. Picking, choosing and selectiveness are the order of the day. Asked about her beliefs, Marilyn Monroe replied, "I just believe in everything—a little bit."[16] Many Christians are only slightly different. Doctrinal dilettantism and self-service spirituality are all part of the trend toward an effete gourmet godliness.

### Go for the Big Prizes

Exploiting pluralization is another of those assignments in which you will need to keep a close check on your agents. Experience here has shown that true "pavement artistry" is likely to degenerate into dirty tricks. This is because pluralization has worked itself out so outrageously in the more extreme cases, and these are easier (and more entertaining) to imitate.

Your colleague in San Diego, for instance, once submitted a paper showing that an interesting effect of pluralization was the increase in rental services. He listed them from the yellow pages, from "rent a pet" to "rent a professional party guest/quarreling couple" ($125 per evening, "gives everyone something to discuss"). At least he was using his initiative—unlike some of the dull apparatchiks we have—and he had an occasional bright insight. As he pointed out, the offer of risk-free ways of keeping emotional investment low is the direct result of pluralization. But his recommendations were preposterous. We put him to work on a tougher assignment, one less conducive to such child's play.

Instruct your agents, as I have stressed to you, that they have pushed pluralization far enough at the level of things. Our goal now is to encourage pluralization at higher levels, so that it produces side effects in relation to places, tasks, values, relationships, societies, and finally beliefs. If they devote too much energy dabbling around at the lower levels, they'll miss what is important at the higher ones.

The Director, as you know, deplores the lack of economy in overkill. He has stipulated that pluralization should not be rushed. There are built-in human and social forces to reverse it if it becomes too extreme. Touch off these and you chance setting in motion a counter-trend, a sort of retrorocket which could waste much of our work.

It's well known, for instance, that part of what prompted the health-food craze was excessive junk food. Too much sexual permissiveness inevitably rebounds in a new Puritanism *(The Joy of Celibacy* predictably following *The Joy of Sex).* If pluralization rebounds similarly, there will be a powerful compensating trend in religion toward moral authority and social unity. If this rebound ever happens, it could with some skill be manipulated toward our ends. But it would be a pity not to ride the wave of pluralization right onto the beach.

Once you've grasped the distinctive workings of pluralization stand back and see how secularization, privatization and pluralization all work together. When secularization and privatization have finished their task, every religion has lost its power. When pluralization has done, each has lost its uniqueness too. Secularization is the body blow, the relentless stamina-sapping punch that leaves the adversary on his feet but finished. Privatization and pluralization are a two-punch combination guaranteed to put him down.

***P.S.*** I gather that before you leave England finally the Director is sending you down to interview the Old Fool, as he contemptuously calls him. There is much more than dismissive ridicule in that title. It's a recognition that he and people like him are among the most dangerous of Christian exceptions. Their entire stories are a living reversal of our Operation. They have virtually backed into faith through a long process of disillusionment with the very fantasies by which most Christians are enthralled. To make matters worse, the Old Fool brings to his faith a comic vision of the frailty and absurdity of life. He thinks this allows him to peep impudently around the corners of the world's mesmerizing triumphs and pronounce them laughable and less then final.

The Director is sending you, however, for an important reason. The role of the media will be central in your work in Los Angeles, and there are few people alive who understand it as well as the Old Fool. Fortunately, he is misunderstood and ignored by his own people, but you need only listen to him carefully, especially to his views on the fantasy-creating power of the media, to see how your strategy should proceed.

In this case, know your enemy and know what your enemy knows and you'll know the best and worst of the church in an afternoon. The insights his own side won't use, we will—against them. The Old Fool is more dangerous than a score of other exceptions, but "10-10-80" still applies.

# MEMORANDUM
# 6

**SUBJECT:**
## EUROPEAN-STYLE
## CONFUSION
**FROM:**
DEPUTY DIRECTOR,
CENTRAL SECURITY COUNCIL
**TO:**
DIRECTOR DESIGNATE,
LOS ANGELES BUREAU
**CLASSIFICATION:**
ULTRA SECRET

■

Have you heard the current definition of an economist? Someone who sees something working in practice and wonders if it can be made to work in theory. Such casting around is hardly exclusive to economics. Few areas are more confusing, in fact, than the debate surrounding the fate of religion in the modern world.

"Something is happening here," growled Bob Dylan in the 1960s, "but you don't know what it is. Do you, Mister Jones?"[1] That could be the text for much of the debate surrounding the three pressures I have outlined. That something of profound importance has happened to religion is almost beyond doubt. But precisely what it is and how to grapple with understanding it are another matter, one that has rolled in a fogbank of confusion and disagreements.

All this is to our advantage, and we have not only exploited it but actively promoted it. Let me now show you how efficiently our plan is working out in practice.

## Cashing In on Credulity

The Department of Counter-Apologetics is the toughest and most purely theoretical of all our divisions, so your training there will not have stooped to include much on disinformation. It will only rarely have entered your work until now, but it must inevitably come into play at this stage. Let me introduce it here to show how we have followed up the three main pressures of modernization.

The best secular examples of disinformation are those which have been blown up to become counterparts of apocalyptic religious myths (such as the recurring panic over successive anti-Christs and other finely spun conspiracy theories). Conspiracy in itself can easily become a sort of religion. But quite apart from this, the religious component is ideal in all disinformation. It imports into the process a sense of absolutism which inflames the motivations and hardens the justifications.

The actual precedent which the CSC had in mind when they met just prior to World War 1 was *The Protocols of Zion,* published in Russian in 1905 by the religious mystic Sergei Nilus. It purported to be reports of the First Zionist Congress in Basel in 1897, divulging plans for disrupting Christian civilization and establishing a world state run by Jews and Freemasons. Befuddling popular opinion with alcohol, corrupting womanhood and fomenting economic distress were among the dark designs allegedly revealed. In sum, it warned the world of an "international Jewish conspiracy."

The book was actually the grubby work of the tsarist secret police, who fabricated it as a tool for anti-Semitism and anti-liberalism. It happened to be a forgery of the stupidest sort, blatantly plagiarized from an obscure text tirading against something quite different. However, and this is why it was interesting to the Council, it struck such a responsive chord socially and religiously that it flourished despite complete discrediting.

You can see this religious component clearly in Nilus's rationale for publishing it even though he knew it was apocryphal. He contrived his own sly justification thus: "For the sake of our faith God can transform the bones of a dog into sacred relics; he can also make the announcement of truth come out of the mouth of a liar."[2]

With religion to rationalize these contortions of the soul, little extra momentum was needed to get the big lie rolling. In Nazi Germany the book went on to outsell everything but the Bible; in the U.S.A. it was believed and published by Henry Ford. From there it eventually became a semi-religious apocalyptic myth, and its path was strewn with havoc. It has been said that those papers have cost the lives of hundreds of thousands, and that more blood and tears cling to their pages than to any other fraudulent document in the world's history.

There you have a crude but very effective example of the religious use of disinformation—deliberately false in order to influence minds, consciously religious in order to inflame hearts. Mere propaganda, by contrast, lacks this precision and potency.

At that pre-World War 1 meeting, when the Council began to deliberate on the optimum way to follow up the impact of modernization, it seemed the only question was the choice of tactics. The conditions for disinformation appeared ideal. The modern world, as George Bernard Shaw was later to point out, was becoming as credulous as the medieval world, except about different things. Human beings have always relished a good story, and relished thinking it true. Therefore, in a credulous age when gullibility was becoming limitless, it would be nothing to concoct some untruth and let it masquerade as gospel. There is no lie some press secretary or newscaster will not confirm as true.

Disinformation flourishes especially well in the confused and anxious conditions caused by war, revolution and economic uncertainty. This has been demonstrated recently in the Cold War, when fear, rumor and misrepresentations have been rife. The Council's early thinking about following up modernization was this: *What the Russian revolution and Communism were later to become to Western capitalism, secularization and secularism might be to Western Christianity.* How could we cash in on the conditions of antagonism and alarm? Could it be that just as Jesuits, Freemasons and Jews had each become scapegoats for conspiracy theories, we could portray secular humanism as the new conspirator for world domination?

At that stage, as I said, the Council's only question was the tool and the tactics. Should they use "white" disinformation (where the authorship and source is open) or "black" (where the attribution is false or misleading) or "gray" (where it is unclear)? Should they use letters, telegrams, reports or memoirs?

It was in the course of this discussion of tactics that their thinking suddenly crystallized. The goal itself was partly wrong. Phobia about secular humanism could be an effective tool with a certain type of person (it's currently working wonders as the number one bogeyman on the agenda of American conservatives), but as an overall strategy it had several weaknesses.

The first two related to the weakness of all falsely planted information, such as the "Hitler diaries." It is liable to be exposed in the end, whether sooner by counter-intelligence or later by courts of law and historians. (Truth will eventually out, the Director says, not because people are honest but because they like to catch liars.) And second, as is the case with many cloak-and-dagger operations, over-reliance on false plants eventually attracts unnecessary attention. Look at the CIA. Hardly a politician dies or a tin-pot regime collapses without someone blaming the "Company." The free world's liberating tool has become the whole world's lightning rod.

The third weakness concerned the risk of using secular humanism in particular. It might easily be used to whip up a sort of Cold War fanaticism in a spiritual mode, but that would only harden Christian attitudes and stiffen Christian resolve. This was the last thing we wanted.

The sort of disinformation we needed was not a false plant claiming something which had never happened, but a smoke screen obscuring what had. The effectiveness of secularization and its superiority over secularism lay in its subtle and invisible working. Secularism was inflammatory and antagonistic, whereas secularization was seductive. If American conservatives were oblivious to the difference between secularism (comparatively weak in the U.S.) and secularization (comparatively strong), so much the better. We needed a style of disinformation to match the iron-fist-in-a-velvet-glove of secularization.

The Council decided to see how the Department of Propaganda and Disinformation would deal with the problem. The question was put to them: How should we follow up the impact of the three pressures of modernization? In particular, how should we do so in a way which would lead not to fanaticism but to defeatism, toward complacency and away from commitment?

**The Chosen Follow-up: A Double-Pronged Thrust**
For the reasons the Council had foreseen, P and D advised against any attempts to plant some elaborately concocted untruth. The way secularization was working itself out in Europe was different from the way it was working itself out in America; our response should be flexible, based on a recognition of this. Where we were exploiting the pressures of modernization to effect the *virtual collapse* of the church (because of its low spiritual and social vitality, as in most of Europe), we should follow that up by creating *confusion* around what had happened; but where the pressures of modernization were effecting only a *vital change* in the church (because of its high spiritual and social vitality, as in the U.S.A.), we should follow that by creating *counterfeit* forms of religion which would be quite as lethal to true faith as no faith at all.

This maneuver has been singularly effective. Where we have achieved maximum damage, our approach has been to create confusion in order to disguise what has happened. But where we have achieved minimum damage, our approach has been to exploit the weaknesses to create counterfeits and make the most of an incomplete job.

The first approach has come to be known as European-style confusion because that is where it was perfected. But it can be applied anywhere that certain conditions are present. It's been our approach in those parts of North America which have proved most susceptible to secularization. I'm thinking particularly of the academic world and related fields such as the press and the media. They are often considered to be more "European" (that is, more liberal and secular) in their mentality. "Let's face it," a leading American journalist wrote recently, "we reporters have very little to do with Middle America. They're not *our* kind of people."[3]

This first approach will seem heavily theoretical at first. That will will be no problem to you, though to those of your agents not trained in counter-apologetics it might be as head-spinning as secularization itself. The tactic is necessarily theoretical because its primary aim is to sabotage Christian *thinking,* but the confusion it creates serves to mask two highly practical matters. One of these is the extent of the devastation we have caused already. (Isn't decline taken for granted in Europe now?) The other is the direction in which we are manipulating the trends. Far from creating the secular, post-Christian Europe of popular mythology, we are actually working toward a world that is essentially pre-Christian and pagan—and far less rational and liberal than most people expect. Leaving aside your personal preferences, nothing could be more practical than that.

It's amusing that intelligence work is often described only in 007 terms, as if it were all guns, gadgets, glamor and girls. The bread-and-butter research of the "burrowers" has never made the headlines; it's the "pavement artists" who have the most fun. But the Bond stuff is rare. The real priority, in fact, is thinking, and an Aston Martin is a good deal less useful than a chess-playing mind. Intelligence and counter-intelligence are basically a battle of wits; the winner is the one who anticipates his enemy's intentions better. Christians are paying through the nose for their current refusal to think. Chase games rather than chess games would seem to be their preference today. So be it. Again our gain. .

## A Smoke Screen around Secularization

You will remember my insistence that secularization is not the same thing as secularism. It is not a philosophy; it is a process which has actually happened. But to say that is deceptive, because the implications of this so-called neutral process or objective event can be twice as damaging as that of the most overtly hostile, anti-Christian philosophy. The volcano has blown, and the geography of traditional society is altered forever. Christians therefore have a vital interest in understanding and evaluating secularization, just as we have in making sure they don't. It is up to us to see that their awareness and analysis of secularization remains as confused and uncertain as possible.

During the famous riots in Chicago at the time of the Democratic Convention in 1968, Mayor Richard Daley announced to the press: "Gentlemen, get the thing straight once and for all. The policeman isn't there to create disorder, the policeman is there to preserve disorder."

His malapropism could be our maxim. How have we achieved this? Mainly by managing to quarantine the discussion in academic circles and by promoting so imprecise and general a use of the word *secularization* that it has become a rag-bag term referring to everything and nothing. As we saw earlier, because of the resulting confusion, some people have despaired of the word and abandoned the discussion altogether. Others have become so waylaid in unraveling the tangle that they will never get anywhere.

This confusion acts as a smoke screen around secularization and obscures a number of simple points, each of which would need to be clear for a Christian breakthrough in understanding. Propaganda and Disinformation can be relied on to maintain the confusion at the following points.

## Confusion One: Distorting Description

If secularization is basically something which has happened, then the first question Christians should be asking is: What exactly has happened? What are the facts of the matter? Only once they know what has happened can they decide to welcome it or regret it, toast it or lament it. With confusion here, either we can disguise the fact that anything significant has happened, thus delaying a response of any kind (which is very damaging to faith), or we can distort and exaggerate what has happened, so that secularization is seen as a *fait accompli* and no response will seem possible or worthwhile (very discouraging to faith).

There are a few dangerous pockets of Christians who have identified their role in the world as "agents in place" behind enemy lines. Do not underestimate them. They recognize that their job is to secure and send back information. They, unlike most Christians, are working from the situation *as it is,* not from what they would like it to be or fear that it may become. They are rejecting impressions, hunches and opinions as irrelevant and pressing for accurate information. Accurate information is precisely what we must deny them.

John Milton held that opinion in good men is but "knowledge in the making."[4] He did not anticipate the twentieth century. Caught between science and television, the one specializing and the other vulgarizing, modern opinions (especially in the form of polls) have more to do with the marketing of ignorance than the making of knowledge. Sounded more, they are sifted less. Much nearer the mark today is Samuel Butler's dictum: "The public buys its opinions as it buys it meat, or takes its milk, on the principle that it is cheaper to do this than to keep a cow. So it is, but the milk is more likely to be watered."[5]

Lazy thinking and mass-produced opinions are only elementary ways of distorting opinion. But they pave the way for surer methods such as playing on people's cherished hopes and deep-seated fears. Do this, and even the most moderate observers will allow their picture of events to be colored.

Take the case of the celebrated reporting by *The New York Times* on the fate of Petrograd in 1917. There was no suggestion of any falsely planted information, and the paper's liberal credentials were impeccable. But one historian later summed up the paper's performance:

In the course of little over two years the *New York Times* reported the fall of Petrograd six times, announced at least three times more that it was on the verge of capture, burned it to the ground twice, twice declared it in absolute panic, starved it to death constantly, and had it in revolt against the Bolsheviks constantly, all without the slightest foundation in fact.[6]

Writing about the same event, Walter Lippman, himself a journalist, commented: "The news about Russia is a case of seeing not what was, but what men wished to see."[7] Play on hopes and fears, and not only will misinformation creep in; it will be willingly accepted by those who should know better. Self-induced disinformation, if you like.

The simplest way to confuse Christians over the issue of secularization is to see that they distort its history. Rewriting history has always been an excellent way of improving one's fortunes. As Butler observed at another time, "Although God cannot alter the past, historians can."[8] This is effortless for us to set in motion but very difficult for them to know how to stop, and curiously the advocate of secularization is as likely to fall in this trap as the opponent. Both stumble on the novelty and freshness of secularization and, in their attempts to state it, both tend to exaggerate its distinctiveness. The former in the hope that it may be accepted, the latter that it may be rejected.

A good example is the suggestion that there was a religious "golden age" from which secularization has caused so sharp and drastic a fall that recovery is out of the question. A real present (which is highly secular) can be falsely contrasted with an imaginary past (which is highly religious). It's quite ludicrous and unhistorical, but the stuff of which invaluable myths are made.

Take a period like the seventeenth century in England, "the golden age of Puritanism." Granted, the Puritan revolution reached its zenith then. But at the same time the sale of almanacs exceeded those of the Bible, and for all the intense spiritual devotion and theological discussion of the period, superstition, astrology and witchcraft were rife.[9] It was hardly a consistent spiritual age, let alone a golden age. Yet like earlier periods (such as the twelfth or fifteenth centuries), it is convenient to use in suggesting that prior to secularization all was well in the world of faith.

A variation on this is to use different standards of measurement for the present from those used for the past. "True Christianity," you suggest with a hint of flattery, "needs to be measured according to high standards of orthodox beliefs and consistent behavior." Under the guise of such a compliment you can then measure modern faith by impossibly high standards and pronounce it incurably secular. The demoralized believer fails to see that if such stiff grading were applied to the church of the past, the sole Christian left would be Christ.

Dramatize secularization through distorting history, and you achieve two things at once. You confirm the skepticism of the disbeliever and reinforce the discouragement of the believer.

### Confusion Two: Rerouting Resistance

A second point of confusion occurs where Christians should be trying to assess secularization in order to know what to resist. But because secularization is not a rival ideology or an alternative religious belief, they cannot see that it has consequences which are more far-reaching and damaging than if it were.

In spite of the mortal danger which modernization represents to the Christian faith, you will notice that the idea of *resisting* secularization is not even on the agenda of most Christians, even apologists. Secularism, yes. You could find a library on that. But not secularization.

For the majority of Christians, this blind spot is due to the weaknesses I covered in an earlier memo. Christians have no feel for the social dimension of faith, and no tool to analyze culture from the vantage point of ordinary experience. They might manage to detect secularism (or any hostile philosophy or religious belief), but because secularization is a process, it passes undetected across their spiritual radar screens.

We can hardly take credit for that sort of folly. But there are other forms of confusion to which we can contribute directly. For example, the confusion in the social sciences over what is scientific has helped divert Christians from getting to the central implications of secularization.

Our approach here has been to keep those outside the social sciences from getting in, and to keep those inside from getting out. The great majority of Christians avoid the social sciences like the plague, quite convinced that these disciplines are dangerously subversive, unsettling both to faith and morals. The present standing of the social sciences, the murkiness of its jargon and the open skepticism of its early days all contribute to this.[10] "Comparative religion makes men comparatively religious," observed Ronald Knox of the problem in a milder form. Taken further, these disciplines are a debunker's delight, and to represent them as such is not difficult. After all, wasn't Marx a sociologist?

Among Christians of the academic sort, we can take the opposite tack. To be truly scientific, they must be objective and unbiased, putting aside personal prejudices (and presuppositions) and pursuing truth in a detached and value-free manner. Insulate them in the scientific community. Make them painfully aware of the prejudice and ignorance of their brethren in the church. Put them in the position of having to prove themselves to secular colleagues by demonstrating their commitment to detachment. Above all else, encourage them to put such an emphasis on objectivity (a necessity of scientific method) that their counterbalancing emphasis on responsibility (a necessity of Christian life and thought) is ruled out.

We will have succeeded when we have them straining hard to be respectably scientific and never getting 'round to being anything else. People like this become so eager to observe that they never judge, so reluctant to be biased and partisan that they dare not be critical and committed. They remember which discipline they are in, but not whose disciple they are.

The net effect will be that those most likely to resist won't know of the danger, while those who know of the danger will be least likely to resist. Again we win either way.

## Confusion Three: Cordoning Off Confession

A third point of confusion is extremely important: keeping them lost in the labyrinth of worldliness. As you may know, even their New Testament has no word for *culture;* the nearest is *world (kosmos).* Christians are trained to see and resist the world as self-centered society which stands against the Adversary. Thus if they had their wits about them, they might realize that an understanding of secularization could be used, like Ariadne's thread, to lead them out of the labyrinth. It would enable them to see when and where they were compromised and in collusion with the world of their day.

This raises the question of Christian corrigibility, the openness to being corrected which, in principle, Christians are supposed to have. This would be a most pernicious spiritual and intellectual trait were it not for one thing: It is rarely practiced. Another magnificent irony. One of the defining features of their becoming Christians is their willingness to face up to being totally in the wrong, yet many Christians never seem to admit to that possibility again. Or at least, if they confess things spiritual and moral, they rarely confess things intellectual and cultural.

In the case of secularization, willingness to identify and confess compromise would correct their shortsightedness and cut them loose from cultural entanglement. We have worked to prevent this. Most Christians, as I've indicated, are blissfully unaware of secularization. For the few who do understand it, our work has been to ensure that the connection between secularization and worldliness is never made. Secularization must be seen as a purely technical term and a sociological matter, while worldliness must be left as a theological term and a purely spiritual matter, one that is heavy with values and judgments that have no place in science.

There is a half-truth in this, of course. No one can properly judge what they have not properly observed, and the proper business of science is observation rather than judgment. On the other hand, once accurate observations have been made, it is entirely proper to use them to make the best judgments possible. Certainly, Christians would always need their own Christian criteria by which to assess worldliness (which is hardly a scientific category). What is fortunate for us is that they don't take the massive evidence for secularization as an inducement to try.

This is surprising since the very meaning and history of the term would invite such an effort. Secularization comes from the Latin word *saeculum* ("age"), which was used in Christian Latin to speak of the world, as opposed to the church. Thus right under their noses, there is a potentially explosive precedent for using the term to describe trends far older and wider than modern secularization.

For our purposes, I have reserved the term *secularization* strictly for describing what has happened as a result of modernization. But in your general research you will discover that it has also been used in the broader and older sense—*wherever the final effect of secularization is worldliness.* You will appreciate that seen this way, modern secularization is merely a new and particularly potent form of ancient worldliness.[11] But we don't want it to be seen this way and have made every effort to prevent them from making the connection.

Recognition of extreme worldliness is dangerous because it creates the risk of "reformation on rebound." We've had a number of public fiascoes to learn from. A good example was the advanced worldliness of the late medieval papacy. The more shocking it became, the more likely it was to shock people into seeing that something was wrong. Take the case of Thomas Linacre, physician to Henry VIII, who gave up medicine in his later years to join the church. Reading the Gospels for the first time, he declared: "Either this is not the Gospel, or we are not Christians."[12]

Similarly, Erasmus viewed the papal spectacle after the invasion of Bologna by Pope Julius and asked whether Julius was the successor of Jesus Christ or Julius Caesar. "If the bad men at Rome make the church to be no church," he added, "then indeed we have no church."[13] You can see how this sort of remark could agitate the consciences of Christians.

Such advanced secularization, in the earlier sense of the word, was vintage worldliness. But as you can see from these incidents, if you push worldliness too far, it can rebound into repentance and reformation. This is why Burckhardt argued that, paradoxically, it was Martin Luther who "saved the papacy."[14] The Renaissance papacy, he observed, was well on the way toward becoming a secularized city-state. As such, it would never have been more than a third-rate temporal power. Having chosen to live by the sword, it would probably have perished by the sword. Certainly, it could never have commanded the obedience of Italy, let alone the wider world. That process was unfortunately arrested. By judging the papacy, Luther saved it.

Since then we have worked on our technique for pushing Christianity into extreme worldliness without provoking reformation. It pivots on always having ready a compelling alternative. Then, if the extreme worldliness of the church shocks people awake, the contrast that strikes them is not between Christian origins and their historical outworkings (an insight that might provoke reformation) but between the awful state of the church and some more appealing alternative.

Take the case of the French church in the eighteenth century. Its worldliness was so extreme that the question *How Christian is Christendom?* could only have the most humiliating response. Like Comte's secular religion, it was virtually "Catholicism minus Christianity."[15] This time, no reformation followed because the moment had been anticipated and the alternatives were ready—rationalism for those who rejected the church's stance on intellectual freedom, socialism for those who rejected her stance on social justice. The result was 1789, not reformation but revolution, and the talk was of strangling the last king with the guts of the last priest. Since then the link in France between atheism and the drive for freedom and justice has been almost indestructible.

Have no illusions that this was effortlessly achieved. For a while it was touch and go, as you can see from the lives of many French thinkers for whom the element of negative reaction to Christianity was critical. Edgar Quinet, for instance, came uncomfortably near to Burckhardt's assessment of Luther when he wrote: "Voltaire is the destroying angel sent by God against his sinful Church with the weapons of the Christian spirit."[16] Renan went further, imagining Christ actually saying to him: "You must leave me if you would be my disciple."[17] Even Voltaire was tottering. At the age of twenty-seven, he complained aloud to Christ, "I am not a Christian but that is to love thee the better."[18]

Disappointed love? Perhaps, but it shows how thin was the line between spiritual reformation and secular revolution. That is the one flaw in extreme worldliness. It is not necessarily terminal. Let it become an issue in itself, and it will lead as often to the church's reformation as to its rejection. That is the distinct advantage for us in concentrating on the narrow, safely scientific, understanding of secularization. That secularization is worldliness must be disguised either by keeping Christians ignorant of it altogether or by keeping it in a scientific compartment so separate from spiritual worldliness that the fateful mating of insights never occurs.

## Confusion Four: Camouflaging the Challenge

There is one method of confusion which will come easily to you with your training in ideas and which has been central to our approach. Secularization, as I have sought to make abundantly clear, is not a philosophy but a historical *reality* which has happened to modern societies over the last two hundred years.

Secularization theory, however—the way in which secularization is analyzed and explained—is a very different kettle of fish. Facts never speak for themselves, so some interpretative frame is obviously necessary and proper. But from the start the course of secularization theory has been swollen and muddied by a flood of alien philosophical assumptions, making it one part scientific description and three parts philosophical evaluation.[19]

Strictly factual descriptions of secularization would be one thing for the Christian to handle, although I have shown you their problems there. But the descriptions are further confused when they are mixed with perspectives alien to the Christian faith. Finally, confusion is compounded when the resulting theories masquerade as scientific and neutral.

In short, some variety of undiluted secularism (the philosophy) gets mixed with secularization (the process) to produce secularization theory. What has actually happened—a matter of fact—gets interpreted by evolutionary theory (or Marxism or whatever)—a matter of a framework. In practice, therefore, secularization theory not only refers to something which has happened; it also refers to something which, for philosophical reasons, is stated and assumed to be progressive and irreversible.

A straightforward description of secularization has implications for the Christian which are demanding but not essentially hostile. Once alien assumptions are smuggled in, however, even the bare statement of secularization can be used as a tool of counter-Christian beliefs, whether they are skeptical, indifferent or hostile.

Logically, the believer has every right to challenge these alien assumptions, either because they pretend to be scientific and neutral, or because the Christian disagrees with them in light of Christian assumptions.

It is in our interest to camouflage the presence of these stow-away assumptions. If Christians don't notice them, they will be influenced by them without realizing it, growing either unduly discouraged or unduly enthusiastic. Even if they do sense the threat inherent in the assumptions, we can work to make them angry or defensive so that they will throw out the true facts along with the false framework. Either way they will eventually come to see themselves in the same perspective and categories as their critics see them.

Do you know the old trick of inculcating the outlook of the "superior" into the "inferior" so that the "inferior," coming to see himself through the "superior's" eyes, actually sees himself as inferior? He is then doubly victimized, first by the "superior" and then *by his own view of himself*. Subject Christians to enough disinformation and this is what happens to them. Just as the Jewish woman victimizes herself when she grows ashamed of the shape of her nose, or the Black when he regrets the color of his skin, so we have modern Christians most captive when they accept the secularist assessment of their faith.

The whole strategy of European-style confusion can be summed up by saying that in spiritual war, as in war generally, the first casualty is truth; and that self-induced disinformation is the subtlest form of deception. Understanding these tactics will be natural for you, just as they will be tortuous for some of your agents. For both reasons I won't add more, but you can see how the net effect of disinformation is confusion and an undermining of morale.

Christians would need to be clear at each point to make an effective response to secularization. But their confusion and demoralization are now so total that most of them see no problem, and those who do can't work out what it is. Such confusion is the ideal smoke screen to conceal secularization. Our progress toward the pre-Christian, pagan world of tomorrow is astonishingly smooth. And Mister Jones still hasn't a clue.

**P.S.** I glanced over the transcript of your interview with the Old Fool. I see he's as trenchant as ever about television's being inimical to truth and ideas. ("I don't think people are going to be preoccupied with ideas. I think they are going to live in a fantasy world where you don't need any ideas.") People think he's referring simply to the content of programs or to the consensus among the program makers. But what he's talking about is the very concept and medium of television itself. A far more radical notion.

Follow his reasoning to the end, and you'll see why the death of truth and the captivity of the church are inseparably linked and why L.A. has the ideal cultural conditions for propagating the triumph of the image. Whether this is video or graven matters little to us.

# MEMORANDUM 7

**SUBJECT:**

## AMERICAN-STYLE COUNTERFEITS

**FROM:**
DEPUTY DIRECTOR,
CENTRAL SECURITY COUNCIL
**TO:**
DIRECTOR DESIGNATE,
LOS ANGELES BUREAU
**CLASSIFICATION:**
ULTRA SECRET

■

It has long been a joke among military strategists that any war between China and the Soviet Union would go like this: The Soviets would take a hundred thousand prisoners on the first day, half a million on the second, and a million and a half on the third, only to surrender on the fourth day—overwhelmed by the number of their captives.

The second of our two approaches for following up the pressures of modernization works much like that. The first, or European-style approach, you remember, is applied in regions such as France and Britain where the church's spiritual and social vitality is low. There we have exploited modernization to effect what by former standards is the virtual collapse of the church. This, as I explained, would also apply to more secular parts of the United States, such as the academic world. The approach is largely theoretical, but the goal and the gains are practical.

The second, or American-style approach, is practical from the very beginning: the creation of counterfeit religions. This is generally applied in regions such as the greater part of North America where the church's spiritual and social vitality is high. There we have exploited modernization to effect what by former standards is a vital change in the church.

The tactic works like this: In times of comparative strength the church makes many converts. It is up to us to see that these converts turn out to be as embarrassingly awkward and unmanageable for them as a horde of Chinese captives would be for the Soviets. This we do by multiplying counterfeit religion and compromising the integrity of the new converts from the outset. The more the messier, as it were.

What do I mean by counterfeit religion? Perhaps not what you'd suppose. P and D have ensured that Christians use the term in a strictly limited way that prevents them from seeing the counterfeits Christians themselves are circulating. I am not referring to alternative religious beliefs nor to spurious subjective experience (although the element of counterfeit is crucial in them too). I am not even referring to the counterfeiting of Christian religion on an individual level. I am speaking of counterfeit Christian religion on a collective or social level. You will quickly see what I mean.

Fortunately, clear, confident Christian attitudes toward other religious beliefs are out of fashion in today's world. (This is why we have recently been able to shut down so many of our counter-apologetic divisions.) Alertness to counterfeit religion at an individual level has also diminished. But what is far more extraordinary is that few Christians have ever really been alert to our counterfeiting of religion on a collective level.

As with counterfeit individual religion (such as Pharisaism, legalism, hypocrisy, cheap grace), counterfeit collective religion pivots on the age-old struggle between faith and natural religion, between the "new nature" and the "old nature," between "the power of God" and the pull of "fallen nature's" gravity, as they put it. In other words, where the spiritual force of conversion directly confronts the natural forces of reversion. We must ensure that in each case the latter wins; that is, that the church conforms to the spirit and shape of the world rather than being transformed and transforming, that Christians revert to their old ways rather than being converted to new ones. I have already described the mounting levels of worldliness involved in subversion (from culture-blind to culture-bound to culture-burnt). The trick is to keep the counterfeit so close to the real thing while the church is passing through these levels that only a trained eye could tell the difference.

Let me illustrate this from the United States. Among the other advantages of working there is the marked absence of trained eyes. American popular religion has parted company with serious thinking for so long that many believers could spot only the crudest and most careless of counterfeits. Indeed, serious thinking in American popular religion must be the most valuable commodity on earth. It certainly seems to be the scarcest.

Be that as it may, the awkward thing about American religion is that, while vitally changed through pressures such as the private-zoo factor, it still has a disturbing degree of spiritual and social vigor. (European religion, by contrast, is hardly worth counterfeiting.) We are therefore following up our initial gains in the States by promoting counterfeit religions to capitalize on the weaknesses we've already exposed there. Let me highlight some of our principal counterfeiting campaigns.

### Civil Religion

Civil religion is counterfeit in the sense that it is *religion shaped by the priorities and demands of the political order.* Loyalty to Caesar once again overrides loyalty to Christ.

In its American form, civil religion is that somewhat vague but treasured set of semi-religious, semi-political beliefs and values basic to America's understanding of herself.[1] You can witness it at its most elegant in the speeches of any presidential inauguration, or at its more homespun on any Fourth of July. The American Creed is quite different from the Apostle's Creed. The latter is basically theological, the former political; the latter a matter of sacred covenant, the former of social contract; the latter is highly distinct, the former deliberately vague. But the American Creed is no less deeply held. The charge "un-American" is far more likely to provoke a deep reaction than the charge "heretical."

How have we succeeded in fusing the two creeds? The issue underlying civil religion is a straightforward one which is inescapable in democracies: What is the basis for a nation's unity and legitimacy? The traditional answer has always been to undergird the national and social order with a spiritual and moral base. In European history this was most often supplied by each country's state church.

Americans, however, rejected this solution in principle almost from the start. Having left Europe to escape religious oppression, and arriving to find a diversity of denominations, they separated church and state and built between them Jefferson's celebrated "wall of separation." American Christians supported and welcomed this separation (Jefferson actually used this phrase in writing sympathetically to a Baptist), and therein lay the seed of their present problems.[2] In effect Christians had deliberately given up the right to assert the lordship of Christ over *every* area of their lives. There was now a vital domain—the state—where they had renounced their right to apply their faith consistently. The renunciation was voluntary but it was a fateful step. Christians believed they were safeguarding pluralism, but unintentionally they were establishing secularization by law. American Christianity has had a slightly boxed-in character ever since.

Christians couldn't anticipate the problems which arose later because Christian values and assumptions were originally basic (along with certain Enlightenment notions) to the consensus which held the state together. Denominational specifics may have been kept out, but general Christian values were largely taken for granted.

Two hundred years later, however, the Enlightenment notions remain but the Christian consensus has gone, shattered by an explosion of pluralism and the introduction of secularism.

This is hardly what the early American Christians bargained for,
but it raises the old question with a new vengeance. What is the basis
of American unity and legitimacy? *E pluribus unum* ("out of many
one") may be a stirring national motto, but it is a demanding and
costly ideal. As this dawns on people (often half-consciously) the
way is opened for us to promote the thrust toward civil religion.

Seen from one angle, civil religion is a kind of half-way house.
It stands between what Americans see as two extremes: on one hand
the dangers of a state church, and on the other the dangers of a
public life without any values at all (a "naked public square"). At
first this solution seems useful to both state and church. It helps the
state because, if public values are not to be imposed from above (an
essentially authoritarian solution), they must be nourished from be-
low. It helps the church because it allows it to contribute to public
life, if only in general terms. Civil religion is thus a compromise
solution which allows the church to exist as an entity that is neither
established nor proscribed. Jefferson's wall is porous, as it were,
and some faith seeps through. There is no national god in America,
and it is politic to refer to him occasionally.

Like many compromises, however, the solution is unstable, and
you can expect to see a series of restless and violent swings between
two other extremes. The first extreme is one that is, sociologically
speaking, *idiocy*—the idea that the social order needs no moral
basis. This might be true if the U.S. were a totalitarian country like
the U.S.S.R. But since the country is as free as it is, the outcome
would be plain: a spiritual void and national decline.

Fear of that possibility rears its head in different ways at different
times (the call for "law and order," the condemnation of "all these
illegal aliens," and so on). Whenever it does, it automatically fosters
a swing to the other extreme, the one we are really after—civil religion. For without a doubt, civil religion is indeed an extreme and
not a meek and mild compromise if seen from the correct angle.

Civil religion is an extreme because it is, spiritually speaking, *idolatry.*

Once you see the dynamics of this swing from idiocy to idolatry, you can see that, for American Christians, civil religion is a case of "out of the melting pot and into the fire." As things proceed well, we can push to make civil religion such an unholy alliance of faith and flag that Christian ideals and American interests are welded inseparably. Christ then becomes little more than court chaplain to the U.S. status quo, ringmaster to the American dream. A dire case of "God on their side"? That's not the half of it. Civil religion is idolatry for one reason only—its god is themselves.

## Consumer Religion

Current conditions in America are ideal for breeding civil religion, and the same is true of the second counterfeit: consumer religion. This is *religion shaped by the priorities and demands of the economic order—* service of mammon outstripping service of the Master.

Have you heard the story of Samuel Goldwyn's attempt to secure the film rights to George Bernard Shaw's plays? Seeking to impress Shaw, he put exaggerated emphasis on his concern for cultural excellence and absolute artistic integrity. Shaw listened politely but finally refused.

"No," Shaw said, "there's too much difference between us. You're interested in art. I'm interested in money."

That's worth remembering when you approach the heat and din of the debate surrounding consumer religion. The lines are not always drawn where you would expect. The politics of envy or sour grapes on one side can sometimes seem as strong as the theology of affluence or egotism on the other. Even well-placed denunciations often do little more than harden the identification of the moneychanger with his wares.

Anything as elementally powerful as religion was bound to be commercialized. History is littered with examples. But what religion is supposed to be more at odds with mammon than Christianity? Jesus drove out the moneychangers. The house of prayer was not to be a warehouse for loot. Martin Luther attacked Tetzel's indulgence sale. Grace was being priced out of the market.

Yet such is our success today that consumer religion's true believers are the very disciples of Jesus, those who would pride themselves on being the heirs of Martin Luther and the truest sons and daughters of the Reformation. Driven out of the temple two thousand years ago, moneychangers are now surfacing in America with all the mystique of a lost tribe of Israel and all the methods of Madison Avenue.

We've done this simply by cultural assimilation. Consumer religion is an unholy amalgam of convictions and consumption that creates a sacramental materialism in the name of Christ. Forget for a moment the wild and ludicrous examples—the vulgar direct-mail appeals, the lavish waste of donated funds, the inflated emotional hypes, the crass theologies of success, the self-glorifying building projects, the "holy hardware" and the "Jesus junk." Those are easy to list but really only symptoms. What few people analyze are the forces behind them. They fail to see the powerful undertow of seductive commercial forces in America which are sucking the gospel down. If consumer religion hadn't existed already, some American entrepreneur would have been glad to invent it.

What are the forces behind it? Where these forces are present, as in America, consumer religion seems as natural as motherhood (as you can tell by the shock when it's attacked). Where they are absent, as in the less-developed world, consumer religion can be seen from a distance for what it is—a particularly crass form of cultural captivity.

One contributing force is that same American pattern of church-state separation which has broken up the monopoly powers of the former state churches.[3] As we have seen, what were formerly "established churches" arrived in North America to find themselves "ex-Churches," and in the process they were forced to change their stance from one of coercion to one of competition. With no state law behind it, each church was out on its own, carving out its own market, winning its own clientele, making its own appeal.

In the process churches experienced a marked shift to stances very like those in the laissez-faire capitalist market. They were no longer monopolistic authorities; more and more they acted like marketing agencies. One nineteenth-century critic observed, "Our metropolitan churches are, in general, as much commercial as the shops."[4] But as Tocqueville and others had realized earlier, this was neither new nor accidental.

A second force contributing to consumer religion has been the virtual sanctification of prosperity and success through the American dream. Religion, you remember, has been confined increasingly to the private sphere at the very time when the private sphere has become the sphere of individual gratification and consumption. This special configuration has produced a surge of conspicuous consumption in religious guise.

Notice how a complete set of adaptable principles and slogans has been created ("Whatever the mind can conceive and believe, it can achieve," "Turn scars into stars" and so on). These are designed for plugging into the Apostles' Creed or the American Creed or both. The Good News and the Good Life, the Christian Way and the American Way are serviced under the same franchise.

The result is a spectacle for our eyes and ears. Theologies compete brazenly to rationalize wealth, success and material blessing. Prosperity doctrines gush forth from rallies, radio and television. ("God's got it, I can have it, and by faith I'm going to get it.")[5] Even Psalm 23 has been revised ("The Lord is my banker, my credit is good. . . . He giveth me the key to his strongbox. He restoreth my faith in riches. He guideth me in the paths of prosperity for his namesake").[6] Gutter-to-grace testimonies have become rags-to-riches testimonials, and fantastic expenditure is poured into showcase projects which are flagships for the showman commanders of the new empires.

Without seeing why, thousands of individual Americans are flocking to this Good Life Gospel and thus doing obeisance to capitalism. They even "consume" faith and church memberships as they would vacations or restaurants, and they rise not only from being bank clerks to bank presidents but from being Pentecostals to being Presbyterians or Episcopalians. (Believe it or not, a correlation has been found between denominations and the likelihood of obesity. Episcopalians, like upper-class people generally, being the leanest!)[7]

A third, more recent, force contributing to consumer religion is the highly commercial nature of the American media which are shaping its Christian users. The Soviet Union is typical of the world's authoritarian type of communication system, just as the BBC stands for a more paternalistic type. The other main type of system is commercial, and nowhere has this been developed further than in the U.S.[8] (The average American child, for example, sees over twenty thousand commercials every year and spends more time in front of the television than in the classroom.)[9]

At first sight the commercial system seems the freest. But its hidden snags lie in the remorseless logic of its economics, since first and foremost it is a marketing medium. It requires vast capital, sure results and quick returns, so it has a built-in bias against the small, the risky, the innovative and the controversial. Yes, almost anything can be said on commercial TV, *but only if someone can afford to say it and if one can say it profitably.* In other words, not everything can be said on commercial television. What, for instance, would be the ratings appeal of a Jeremiah or an Amos or of "the offense of the cross"? Commercial television is for profits, not prophets, and the tele-evangelists have been quick to learn the difference.

There is also a fourth factor, a force that is carrying consumer religion right into the big league: Only recently have Christian conservatives moved out of the closet and into the culture. Some of them therefore combine the starry-eyed naivety of a Johnny-come-lately with the insatiable appetite of a Harry-come-hungry. They want to catch up and to make up for lost time. And notice whom they ask to countersign their excesses.

"Why should the Devil have all the good music/art/jobs/success/ life?" they argue reasonably, before shedding the inhibitions of centuries and plunging into freedom like new converts to hedonism. Or, if you ask them how they reconcile all that talk about money with Christianity: "It's easy," one of them explains. "I believe God made the diamonds for his crowd, not for Satan's bunch."[10] Only a towering naivety could think such freedom is a gain.

So we might go on but the point is sufficiently established. Examples of the brash worldliness of consumer religion will be all around you, nowhere more than in southern California. But leave it to others to get bogged down in fascination with the particular examples. Our job is to see broad trends and isolate forces so we can analyze and exploit them. Many of the sternest critics from the other side have failed to analyze the underlying trends. This gives us a critical edge.

Christians overlook the fact that to become a significant market is as much a source of problems as a sign of power. They might have learned from the youth market in the sixties, which was the immediate forerunner of the evangelical market in the seventies. The principle is as follows: the stronger the subculture, the more powerful its commercial potential. The so-called counter-culture came to express its protest and its aspirations in the rock music and blue jeans which became the sound and style of the movement. And in the process a vast new market was created.

Once these things were on the market, however, they could be sold by anyone and bought by anyone. As a result, counter-cultural symbols lost their distinctiveness and became fashionable, then empty and open to manipulation. Who could take radicals seriously when their rhetoric was interrupted by the jingle of a million cash registers? "Every thrust at the jugular," as one of them put it, "brought forth not blood but sweet success."[11]

That was partly why the counter-culture did not succeed. It was co-opted by Madison Avenue. In the end it was not even a permanent subculture, only a way station for youth. We intend to bring the same Midas touch to the current American renewal, so that through the amalgam of convictions and consumption a market is made out of a movement, congregations are turned into customers, and the gospel is groomed to gross well.

This is proving easier than we expected, as a glance at a recent trend in advertising will show you. Bob Hope once told a story about flying across America in a plane which was hit by lightning.

"Do something religious!" shrieked a little old lady across the aisle.

"So I did," he wisecracked. "I took up a collection."

But the relationship between the Bible and the bucks is no joke today. It's big business. It's the right button to push, whether in jest or in earnest. A recent ad in *The New Yorker* ran, "After twenty years of driving Volkswagen religiously, the Reverend Dr. Gray-Smith converted. . . . Le Car has turned millions into true believers." Can you imagine Renault advertising like that in France? In secular Europe their little joke would have all the resonance of a wet cardboard bell.

In America, however, the joke is now told not only behind Christians' backs, but to their faces. You don't need market research to tell you that conservative Christians have a biblical text to justify whatever they do. So how has the Israeli national airline advertised in a leading conservative Christian magazine? "In 10 hours we fly you to where Jesus walked" ran the headline over a shot of Lake Galilee with the text: "Come ye after me, and I will make you to become fishers of men." You've come a long way, baby, to buy that one so solemnly. But the El Al "Pilgrimage Department" winks all the way to the bank.

You can see how the course of consumer religion is Operation Gravedigger in miniature. Late American evangelicalism is partly descended from English Puritanism, but between them are three centuries, two worlds and a complete theology. The earlier movement saw covetousness as the master sin, the essence of the lust of the spirit. Such Puritans were dangerous. They treated riches with a disciplined inner detachment and regarded poverty as infinitely preferable to prosperous worldliness.

Their heirs have neatly reversed this. They see the official master sin (if there is one at all) as the lust of the flesh, not the spirit. Unofficially, poverty and failure are even worse, whereas riches are glorified and equated with blessing. "It is the duty of every man to be a prosperous man," exclaimed a nineteenth-century trailblazer for this truth.[12] "God's will is prosperity," echoes today's tele-priest as he thanks God for his "blessed Cadillac."[13] Such high buffoonery is harmless to us, though an invaluable contribution to the decline of the modern church, if not the West itself. Late American evangelicalism is early Puritanism in its dotage, the Protestant work ethic gone to seed.

American religion has always been known for its sacramental materialism, but with the recent boom and the arrival of the electronic church, it has tools of which Tetzel never dreamed and profits to make a moneychanger blush. Today, what is to be escaped is poverty, not purgatory, and what is for sale is indulgence of another kind. With miracle prayer cloths now sent out by mass mailing and by Protestants, the wheel has come full circle. The co-opting of the Reformation is well advanced. Little wonder that the market in retail religion is bullish. Spiritual renewal means business is booming for the brokers of consumer religion.

**Closed Religion**
America's refusal to have a state church and her extraordinary wealth make her uniquely open to the seductive powers of civil religion and consumer religion. This, as I said, is offensively plain to outsiders, though only because they do not happen to share the same conditions. Watch almost any European programs on American religion (on the electronic church, say, or the Moral Majority), and you'll see how superior outsiders can be. Much of this is sheer hypocrisy. Superiority born of a cultural accident is hardly a moral achievement, though P and D are always able to use the caricatures it creates.

Therefore, as a third example of our counterfeits, let me take a phenomenon which is found in almost all modern countries and which only happens to be more advanced in the U.S. This is closed religion, by which I mean *religion shaped by the priorities and demands of the social order.* The issues behind closed religion and civil religion are similar, but with closed religion the focus is not on society; it is on the interests of the individual. The issue at stake in this case is: What is the source of an individual's meaning and belonging?

Nothing is more characteristic of the modern world than the restless, sometimes desperate, search for meaning and belonging. Sense of some kind, stability of some sort—these are prerequisites for a tolerable life, keeping the specter of irrationality and absurdity at bay. Yet for many people, both meaning and belonging are in short supply today because of the high degree of disintegration in advanced societies.

This lack gives rise to a simple dynamic which is natural for us to harness: *When social chaos, then religious cults.* This is not new. You can see it in the lively religion of the frontier days in nineteenth-century America, or further back in the long succession of extreme millenarian movements in Europe. The principle is the same. Periods of rapid change and social disruption create powerful needs which seek answers in new sectarian groups.

Do you know the so-called hemline indicator of economics? It is the idea that the stock market rises and falls with the hemline, looser financial controls meaning freer and more revealing clothes (and vice versa). Closed religion can be charted much more reliably than that. It was no accident, for instance, that expressions of closed religion mushroomed in the seventies as a direct reaction to the sixties. Freedom! was the cry of the sixties. Freedom from tradition, custom, routine, morals, authority and all that inhibited the spontaneous expression of the autonomous individual in the unbounded moment. That, as we know, led to some ridiculous things. But its value for us was that it created a vacuum which in turn built up a consuming hunger for the very things that had been discarded.

Predictably, there was a rebound—from openness to closure, from virtual anarchy to authoritarianism, from a tolerance of ambiguity to an intolerance of anything but buttoned-down certainty, from a make-it-up-as-you-go-along freedom to a prepackaged form. The liberated generation suddenly woke up and found itself the fatherless generation; and in the ensuing scramble for authority, community, family and home, it showed itself decidedly unparticular.

This is the context of the '70s-style surge of closed religion which reached its climax in Jonestown. But the People's Temple was not altogether the deranged exception many people thought. It was only following to a logical extreme what a whole decade showed in milder ways—and not least the church.

I said to you earlier that we were using two weapons to counter the potential danger of the charismatic movement. Privatization was the first and here (in closed religion) is the second. You may have noticed the sudden somersaults of some of the fringe charismatic groups, for example. One moment they were all for freedom (rejecting one-man ministry, impatient with hide-bound liturgies and traditions, overturning male domination). Then presto, and a thousand mini-popes were strutting around telling their followers what to believe, how to behave, whom to marry, with whom not to associate.

Such swings toward micro-totalitarianism were dressed up properly, of course, sailing under the flags of respectable notions such as authority, discipleship and accountability. But unquestionably they were closed religion, the Christian faith sucked into the black hole of today's vacuum of meaning and belonging.

These three—civil religion, consumer religion, closed religion—are only samples of the counterfeit forms of religion on which we are working. I could mention others, such as common religion (religion shaped by the priorities and demands of popular opinions and feelings) or clan religion (shaped by the tribe or cultural grouping). I could also mention other valuable side effects. Counterfeit religion is an easy way, for instance, of increasing prejudice against Christianity around the world. (If American Christians cannot distinguish between Christianity and Americanism, how can others be expected to do so?) But our aim in them all is the same: to ensure that the church is shaped rather than shaping, reverting to the pattern of its culture rather than renewing its culture after the pattern of the Adversary.

The old, "brooding Dane" saw this beginning more than a century ago. "In every way it has come to this," Kierkegaard wrote, *"that what one now calls Christianity is precisely what Christ came to abolish.* This has happened especially in Protestantism."[14] The only surprising thing about our success is how open and obvious the result has been. "He who travels in the barque of St. Peter had better not look too closely into the engine room," Ronald Knox warned earlier.[15] Our success with her Protestant sister ship is now so total that engine-room affairs have taken over the bridge and spilled out onto the decks.

This concludes my review of the double strategy through which we have followed up the advantages of the three main pressures of modernization. Having seen the pressures operating full force, and our own campaigns to confuse and counterfeit going well, we can turn next time to survey the damage.

**P.S.**   I was telling someone from the Archives Department about the holy hardware (Jesus baby bibs, Christian tea bags, fortune cookies with Scripture texts inside, frisbees with the legend "The rapture is the only way to fly," and so on). Admittedly he's a little thick, but he simply couldn't hoist it in. Would you send him an assortment of the stuff the next time you're over? It would be useful for the archives anyway. In fifty years' time no one will believe it without seeing it.

# MEMORANDUM
# 8

**SUBJECT:**

## DAMAGE TO ENEMY INSTITUTIONS

**FROM:**
DEPUTY DIRECTOR,
CENTRAL SECURITY COUNCIL
**TO:**
DIRECTOR DESIGNATE,
LOS ANGELES BUREAU
**CLASSIFICATION:**
ULTRA SECRET

■

During my time in the Paris bureau, I used to dine regularly with a lieutenant colonel in the French Secret Service who was famed for his passion for two things: *Chateauneuf du Pape* and realism. In terms of the latter, he used to tell a story from World War 2 to make a point. When the German U-boat menace was at its height, the U.S. Defense Department was making every effort to find an effective solution. Among the dozens of suggestions considered, one was from a scientist who recommended boiling the Atlantic until the submarines rose to the surface and exploded. Highly skeptical, a Defense Department official asked the scientist how he proposed to do this.

"I'm paid to have the ideas," the scientist retorted. "You're paid to implement them."

All their proposals, the Lieutenant Colonel warned his staff, had to be practicable. The impractical, however imaginative, were not wanted.

Sweet realism. Would that it were branded on the tiny minds of all our Bureau directors. Intelligence work recognizes only one final law: results. I shudder when I think of the time and energy wasted on harebrained schemes with almost no return. Your former division of counter-apologetics has not been guiltless here. Even your predecessor at Oxford was ridiculously profligate in his efforts to foster a once-for-all, knock-down argument against the Christian faith.

He never achieved it, of course. Doubtless, he'd still be trying if we hadn't sent you to replace him. But his real folly was this. Even if he had managed to contrive the conclusive argument, it still wouldn't have been conclusive for many people. Most people today are not argued out of faith any more than they were argued into it in the first place.

Operation Gravedigger takes this into account and has no such drawbacks. Let us therefore turn from examining the pressures brought to bear on Christianity and look now at the problems these have created for the church. I will begin by outlining the damage to Christian institutions. In later memoranda, I will look at the damage to Christian ideas and to Christian involvement in the world.

**Two Reminders**
As we shift our focus to the specific problems created for the church, you will have to keep in mind two important points. First, these problems are not unique to the Christian church. Other religions have been affected, for example, insofar as they have been modernized too.

Take the case of Transcendental Meditation and the Maharishi Mahesh Yogi. What you see in the West is a streamlined, export model of Hinduism, designed especially for the Western market and even masquerading as a nonreligious "science." The number of Americans who practice TM are minuscule compared with those attending weekly Bible studies, so the importance of TM has been grossly exaggerated by the media, although it does sell reasonably well in the present spiritual climate. Even so, what many of its Western clientele don't realize is the extent of the modernizing job done on it, a job which simultaneously disguises its worst features and abandons some of its better (not least that its teaching was traditionally free of charge!).

What is true of the damage to other religions is true also of other institutions, ranging from the family to the state. Above all, it is true of countless millions of modern individuals (in the compounding of loneliness in modern cities, for example). The modern world has indiscriminately left its mark on all sides. Almost no one and nothing is immune from its shaping power at some point.

If we can conceal this fact from Christians, they'll have a picture which is both distorted and discouraging. Christianity has been among the hardest hit, although not for the reasons some Christians think. The blow seems worse to the church, partly because she was so strong and central before and partly because she was so close to the modern world that she was bound to be hit first. That, in a sense, is the closest thing to a eulogy Christianity will get in the modern world. But not knowing the background, some Christians think that the damage to their faith must be due to an inherent weakness in Christianity itself.

The second point to remember concerns the nature of the damage we're examining. We're not dealing with a crisis of the church's credibility, but a crisis of its *plausibility* (whether Christianity *seems* true, not whether it *is* true). I don't need to tell you the extent of the church's credibility crisis. You instigated part of it. But as I stressed earlier, our concern is to undermine Christian plausibility, to create such a gap between its spiritual rhetoric and its social reality that, whatever it may say, Christianity is bound to seem hypocritical or untrue.

Think of it from the angle of the church itself. The church, you remember, is Christianity's plausibility structure, its so-called pillar and bulwark of the truth. This means that subjective certainty in the

Christian faith will rise and fall, fluctuating according to the fortunes of the church. When the church is consistently and continuously strong, Christianity will seem true. When the church is weak, any certainty anchored in the church will weaken too, and Christianity will seem less true, even untrue.

In the early days, the principle of plausibility worked against us. Christianity in the Roman world grew from a minority to a majority to a monopoly. Thousands jumped on the bandwagon as it did so, especially after the conversion of Emperor Constantine. Christianity seemed to be more true every day, or (to be more accurate) it seemed true to more people every day.

Now, however, plausibility is working for us. Once it was too easy to *believe* for the wrong reasons. Now, as Christendom has crumbled, the church's status in many countries has slipped from a monopoly to a majority to a minority. As a result it is easy to *disbelieve* for the wrong reasons. Whether or not Christianity is true is now irrelevant; to more and more people in the modern world it no longer *seems* true.

Another way to look at it is from the angle of the church's claims. However attractive or coherent they sound in theory, if these claims can be denied in practice, they will not seem true and neither will Christianity.

As I pointed out earlier, our focus in the nineteenth century was on the church's stand on intellectual freedom and social justice. The heart of our attack was not that Christianity was untrue, but that it was unfree and unjust. Marxism, in particular, represented a brilliant shift in tactical offense; it by-passed any effort to pin the charge of intellectual falsity on Christianity and concentrated instead on its failure in terms of social function. Regardless of whether Christianity was obscurantist for the philosophers (the old charge), it was an opiate for the masses and a mask of respectability for those who exploited the masses. This new charge was far more damaging than a hundred clever or "conclusive" arguments about truth.

In the same way, notice how most of the damage caused to Christian institutions today comes from the glaring inconsistency between

Christian principles and Christian practices, between the church's spiritual rhetoric and its social reality, between the claims Christians make and their failure to carry them through consistently. Above all, see how the Adversary's rule (which they trumpet as "the lordship of Christ"), although supposed to be a dynamic ideal in principle, has become a dead letter in practice. The three great pressures of modernization have seen to that. They have opened a yawning chasm between Christian claims and their consequences and so ushered in a plausibility crisis of historic proportions.

Hold in your mind, then, that if Christianity is to seem plausible, its claims would have to be practiced with reasonable consistency. Let us therefore look at the church in the modern world and see how its institutions have fared, particularly in terms of the requirement to make Christ's rule a reality.

### Evacuation from the Public Sphere

It's a generalization, but a sound one, that Christianity has evacuated the public sphere almost everywhere. This has been described in various ways, all centering on the same point: The Christian faith has been disconnected, uncoupled or disengaged from the public world.[1] Even one of the enemy agents, a man who hotly disputes the extent of secularization, has been forced to admit: "Big Government, Big Business, Big Labor, Big Military and Big Education are not directly influenced either by religion or by the Church."[2]

This evacuation has not been a choice the church has made consciously (except for the voluntary separation of church and state in the United States). The obvious reason for this development is secularization, just as privatization is the reason why it has not been noticed. Sector after sector has been successively freed from the influence of the Christian faith, so that for all practical purposes the heartland of modern society is thoroughly secular. The steely grip of the sacred-secular distinction is now a stranglehold.

In relation to the church's previous public influence, there are only two significant exceptions to this general evacuation. Once you examine them, both prove empty. The first is *ceremonial religion,* that which remains of the influence of the previously powerful state churches; the second, which we've already looked at, is *civil religion,* where an indirect and diluted Christian influence on public affairs is still possible despite the deliberate rejection of a state church.

Certainly these are exceptions. Such as they are, they exist in the public world. Religion stops at the boardroom door, the factory gate and the laboratory bench—that's taken for granted. But it is also still taken for granted that you don't solemnize a royal marriage, declare a foreign war, swear an oath in court or inaugurate a president without some traditional religious references.[3]

Such religion plays a part in public life, like icing on a cake or parsley on a steak. But who's kidding whom? European ceremonial religion is Christianity at its emptiest and most occasional, a pageantry machine rolled out for state occasions, an archaic Gothic ornament inspiring rhetoric and nostaglia in a prosaic and hard-bitten age. In Britain ceremonial religion has almost lost its spiritual authority altogether. It now alternates between the lofty detachment of its national role as "the imposing west front of civic religion"[4] and its more engaged, day-to-day stance as the moral footnote of a *Guardian* editorial (each retreat in theological assurance seemingly counterbalanced by an advance in political assertiveness).

Sweden, with even stronger secularization, has taken the process further still. There ceremonial religion keeps alive a flicker of historic nostalgia but serves mainly as a social service station—state-subsidized to see to the "hatching, matching and dispatching" of a population which otherwise lives in scant regard of its claims.

In much the same way, American civil religion is Christianity at its vaguest and most general, a spiritual muzak that has become regulation accompaniment to certain public occasions. (*God* is a crescendo word used by American politicians to lift the last line of their speeches.) I dealt with civil religion in the previous memo, showing how easily it can be exploited to produce counterfeit religion.

Neither ceremonial religion nor civil religion is entirely valueless to Christians, but in terms of any spiritual power each is a devotional intrusion rather than a decisive influence on public affairs. Neither is a true exception to the picture of a general evacuation.

Who can take seriously a faith which claims to speak to all of life but has tamely withdrawn from the areas which are central in modern society? "Jesus is Lord," Christians say, but what do they show? He does not appear to be lord here . . . nor there . . . nor anywhere much where it matters. This almost total evacuation represents a rout of the first order, effectively giving the lie to Christian claims of sovereignty and lordship.

Notice also that both these forms of religion are vulnerable to exploitation (Christ's becoming, as we've seen, court chaplain to the status quo), and both are vulnerable to exposure.[5] Ritual and formality have a see-through flimsiness today, and certain people are falling over themselves in their eagerness to play the small boy who pronounces the emperor naked. In short, whatever is left of Christianity in public we can either manipulate or mock.

### Restriction to the Private Sphere

There have been two broad responses to the general evacuation of Christianity from public life. The first is the majority response, mostly comprising Christian movements at a popular level but including many individuals from higher levels too. This response has been *to accept the restriction of religion to the private sphere.*

We have already examined the trend of privatization and seen its decisive damage to the Christian faith. Secularization, as I've indicated, has been the major force behind the evacuation of Christianity from public life; privatization has been the principal reason why the extent and significance of the evacuation has not been seen. Not only is Christianity restricted to the private sphere, mot Christians like it that way.

A natural result of this is that the forms of faith that have flourished are those best suited to the private sphere. Thus they have been tailor-made for manipulation. In America in the fifties, for example, there was a religious revival which turned out to be little more than a suburban family boom. Spiritual indicators such as church membership, giving and education all soared, but social influence soon sagged.

Membership often turned out to be temporary, superficial and hypocritical. For what reason? Parents were committed more to the idea of their children being churched (or better still, "Sunday-schooled") than to the church itself. They went on their own terms, not Christ's. In addition, most of the churches' booming activities related to the private life rather than the public, so that the church, apart from catering to the family, was socially irrelevant—and shown to be so by the events of the sixties.

One enemy expert warned clearly that so naive and family-oriented a revival was virtually "the second Children's Crusade."[6] Fortunately, he was ignored, but the sixties proved his point. Members of the baby boom graduated from their Sunday schools and their faith at the same time. When they took their stand in the streets of Berkeley, Columbia and Kent State, that naive Christianity was their opponent, not their inspiration.

Decades after the '50s boom, privatized religion is still as useful to us, though the forms have changed. It has come a long way from the innocence and intactness of the world of Eisenhower. Not only are new technologies available to it; new factors such as the preoccupation with survival, are influencing its mood.[7] Unlike their predecessors, today's privatized parents are likely to feel increasingly under seige. Yet they are still glued to the television which simultaneously thrusts in the hostile outside world and offers the best escape from it. For some tips in catering to this present mood, listen to the tele-evangelists. Electronic churchmanship lacks nothing in market research.

Do you appreciate the invidious choice now facing most modern Christians? Should they opt for faith that is a matter of public rhetoric or of private religiosity? The choice is between embracing a faith which is universal and a faith which is real. To the extent that faith goes public and achieves universality, it lacks reality; to the extent that faith goes private, it achieves reality but lacks public bite or social consequence. Christianity has lost its footing in the public square and is on the horns of a vicious dilemma.

### Reduplication of the Public Sphere

The restriction of religion to the private sphere is so widespread that many people overlook a second response to loss of public influence. In this response Christians *attempt to re-enter the public sphere by uncritically reduplicating the stances and styles of the public sphere itself.* At first sight this minority response (faith going public again) might appear threatening to our work, but in the long run it isn't. It uses the tools of the public world and does so on the public world's terms, ending up compromised and captive yet again. To coin a phrase, worldly.

*1. Following the star.* I could cite numerous examples of this but all of them turn on the same principle and lead to the same end. A very clear one is *commercialization,* the result of the church's attempt to re-enter the public sphere by reduplicating the principles and practices of the capitalist market. This is how consumer religion develops and becomes an effective counterfeit. Its uncritical reduplication of the marketplace leaves it sold out to its culture. Undeniably, consumer religion is religion which has re-entered the public world—colorfully, successfully and profitably. Undeniably, too, it has done so only by working in the public world's way.

I needn't add much to what I said about consumer religion in the previous memo, except perhaps to give you one more specific illustration. I'm tempted to take Christian publishing, but instead let me show you the way in which Christians are duplicating the public world's celebrity system.

When Adlai Stevenson was running for the U.S. presidency in the 1950s, he was asked whether the public adulation was doing him any harm. "It's all right," Stevenson replied, "so long as you don't inhale." Today that attitude would be thought of as humility to a fault. Publicity rivals money as the mother's milk of politics. Politicians, it is now said, no longer run for office—they pose. But Christians too have become hooked, inhaling publicity like chain smokers, quite oblivious to the warning on the packet.

The context of this speaks for itself. Modern media offer a novel

power for manufacturing fame. They create an instant fabricated famousness with none of the sweat and cost of true greatness or heroism. And in a highly anonymous society, one which is obsessed with image and impermanence, who can calmly wait for recognition? Fame is the highest of all highs, and publicity—even bad publicity—is the instant fame that by-passes the need for accomplishment or worth. As Oscar Wilde said, "There is only one thing in the world worse than being talked about, and that is not being talked about."

Hence the celebrity, the person who in Daniel Boorstin's phrase is "well known for his well-knownness," the "personality" for whom television is not for watching but for appearing on.[8] As you can see, publishing and the celebrity system overlap here. A "best seller" is becoming the celebrity among books, one which sells well partly because it sells well, the essence of the successful hype.

Whatever happened to that rather awkward saying of Jesus, "Woe to you when all men speak well of you"?[9] Somehow Christians have conveniently forgotten it, particularly Christians in America where the access to the media is greatest. Hence the celebrity system, Christian-style ("A Star Is Born-Again"). Titans from the worlds of politics, sports, music, television and religion stride the Christian stage and screen with an authority born only of their mass appeal. "Following the star" has become the exact opposite of what it was for the three wise men. Today it leads away from Christ, not toward him.

As a young preacher in Indianapolis, Jim Jones (of People's Temple fame) is reported to have thrown his Bible on the floor and yelled at his associates, "Too many people are looking at this instead of looking at me!" Christian celebrities might not go that far. They wouldn't need to. But far more importantly, they wouldn't do the reverse. By definition, celebrities are to be celebrated. Therein lies our chance.

If consumer religion transforms congregations into clientele, its idolizing of celebrities produces a series of fateful switches in focus: from private identity to public image (devaluing inner life and character), from saints to stars (devaluing models of spiritual growth), from followers to fans (devaluing patterns of discipleship), from being gifted to being glamorous (devaluing leadership and spiritual authority), and from wisdom, understanding and experience to endorsements, personal glimpses and slogans (devaluing faith).

Modern man and woman do not live by bread alone, but by every catchword and revelation which comes from the lips and private lives of their heroes. But since such fame is largely based on famousness, these celebrities are living tautologies and the emptiest of heroes. Thus for ordinary people, the consumption of celebrities is like psychological fast food. For Christians, it is not only unnourish-·ing but a slow and deadly poison. Those who live by the image die by it too. And those who worship them are like them.

The contrast here with the Old Fool is plain, and you can see why his one-man war against fantasy would be dangerous if his lead were followed. Look back at the transcript of your interview, and you'll see examples of the sort of subversive impudence I mentioned to you when you first went down to see him.

"If you imagine yourself as a pure sojourner in a world in which a great many people—some of the most influential and perhaps even gifted people—assume that this world is the full story, and you know it isn't, you can't but find their circumstances and behavior and state of mind rather ridiculous."

Even for the celebrity worshiper, such a perspective might be hard to disagree with when stated like that. This sense of incongruity and discrepancy spoils the image for good, and the celebrity can never be seen in the same light again. The small boy has cried out once more, and another embarrassed emperor must hurry home for some clothes.

Fortunately, it is a way of seeing too rare to trouble us. I have pointed out before that effective subversion requires at least two things: the passive acceptance of the masses, and the positive allegiance of a ruling counter-elite. Christian reduplication of the current celebrity system makes this area an obvious tool for achieving the former. "10-10-80" is right on course.

**2. *What's good for General Motors*.**   If commercialization is what occurs when the church uncritically employs the principles and practices of the market, the result of the church's uncritical emulation of the public world's form of organization and administration is *bureaucratization*. Bureau-cracy, literally "desk power," still has a bad popular press today. For many people, it stands for bungling inefficiency, faceless officialdom, interminable delays, endless forms to be filled in and petty humiliations to be endured. Kafka's *Castle* in a thousand variations.

This, however, is old-fashioned bureaucracy, which shambled along until the swelling army of management experts and behavioral engineers moved into streamline and update it. In its modern form, no way of organization and administration is more rational, efficient and characteristic of the twentieth century. Government, business, education and the military all reflect these newer bureaucratic structures. And now so does religion.

It goes without saying that nothing could be further from the needs and aspirations of privatized religion. But bureaucratization caters to a different group of Christians. It therefore complements rather than contradicts the former because it operates at a different level. Privatized religion is mostly (but not exclusively) found at the grassroots level, whereas bureaucratized religion is the result of the reduplication of the modern world at the level of leadership, management and organization.

Bureaucratization is nothing new for the church. The hierarchy of the medieval church was a rationally organized administrative system modeled on that of the Roman Empire. The most obvious recent example of our success in spreading bureaucratic structures is the denomination. Indeed, we've made such strides that only a fool or a true believer still thinks that denominations differ from one another for decisive theological reasons. For all their different traditions, most denominations now resemble each other remarkably closely in structure.[10] They are all cast in the same bureaucratic mold, run by the same bureaucratic logic and confronted by the same bureaucratic imperatives such as public relations, fund raising and lobbying. Watch their day-to-day operations, their hierarchical chains of authority, their external dealings, and what do you see— the "body of Christ" or a pale ecclesiastical version of a multinational corporation?

A less obvious example is the spread of bureaucratic structures in the so-called parachurch ministries, those independent ministries which operate alongside the church. Here you can see the element of reduplication with particular freshness, since many of these groups have risen only in the last generation and among people who previously had a wary suspicion for the ways of the world.

Make no mistake. The parachurch movement is a menace to us. That was why the Director singled it out for attention. He anticipated that contemporary Christianity would be at its most enterprising and energetic here. Here can be found its most potent blend of vision, skill, initiative and dedication. Movements such as evangelicalism, having lost control of the denominational institutions to liberals, would be weak and diffuse without the strong networks and cross-fertilization of the thousands of parachurch ministries. (There are more than ten thousand in the U.S. alone.) These organizations have their people everywhere today. The Third World and the student world, sportsmen and film stars, down-and-outs and "up-and-outs." You name it, they have a ministry for it.

Despite that, we can be confident. In their eagerness to break away from stale and ineffective ways of doing things, they are rushing breathlessly and mindlessly for the latest philosophies, the top consultants and the most effective modern tools. Is there a recent insight, perhaps, from the American Management Association? A new method from the Harvard Business School? The most up-to-date statistics from a research organization? The doors are open, and the rush is on. Like dollar-happy bargain hunters, they are out to streamline their organizations with the best bureaucratic structures that money can buy.

As this trend continues, we can expect them to meet problems at two places. The first is where bureaucracy *fails*. This will not be a case of its being wrong nor worldly from the Christian point of view, but simply of its breaking down in practice. Regardless of the modern streamlining, bureaucracy still has problems. Goals tend to be displaced as means and procedures become ends in themselves; relationships become depersonalized as they flatten out into roles; certain cookie-cutter personality types develop because certain characteristics such as security, loyalty and dependency are emphasized unduly. Each of these developments represents a snag for bureaucracy of any kind; for "the body of Christ" they can become a denial of its truth altogether.

The second problem area is where bureaucracy *succeeds,* but where its success will be on its own terms, terms which will militate against the church. I've already mentioned how bureaucratic structures override distinctive theological differences, such as between congregational-style government and government through bishops. We want the same thing to happen to parachurch ministries; our variant on the old adage that in matters of the spirit, nothing fails like success.

There are early signs that we are making headway. Reliance on the computer is fast replacing reliance on the Holy Spirit. Development is a growing substitute for conversion. Modern personnel descriptions (dynamic, personable, efficient) are crowding out traditional categories, such as preacher or evangelist, and ignoring old-fashioned qualities, such as meekness or humility. Prayer letters are drowning under a deluge of slick appeals for money. "Results" have ousted "fruit" as the yardstick of success, and the matrix of action is no longer worship and fellowship. Instead, a self-perpetuating series of congresses, consultations and committees is orbiting the Christian world, launched, serviced and commanded by a new elite of international consultants. These are the seasoned Christian congressnauts, at home in all the world except at home.

Christians have always shown a curious inability to consider things from a long-term perspective. Most have been blind to the dynamics of a parachurch movement. How else could they fail to see the natural stages of its trajectory?

Put simply, there is first a *man or woman* with a vision of something lacking in the wider church. Next, there are people who share that vision, and gather around the pioneer to support his stand. Then, there is a *movement,* structured and organized to express that vision and thrust it on its way. Finally, after however many years, with the hallowed portrait of the founder smiling down on the boardroom of his or her successors, all there is left is a *monument.* Bureaucracy, in short, helps turn the revolutionary into the routine, the insight into the institution. It's slower and less glamorous than the Midas touch, but just as deadly in the end.

An important part of our game here is bluff. Leaders of parachurch ministries are well aware that to succeed in their task they must feed their contribution back into the local churches. Their job, they say, is to put themselves out of a job. And, of course, they're right. Nothing would arrest bureaucratization faster. But out of many thousands who say this, only a handful do it. Most parachurch ministries clutter the ground long after their days of usefulness are over.

We bluff them by agreeing with them. We urge them to make "service" their motto and their theme song, knowing that service is addictive once it becomes the source of their identity (and income). This is how they get hooked: At first they are needed and they serve. Soon they both need to serve to be needed, and they need needs to serve. Before long, they become experts in service. And, since indispensable servants often become indistinguishable from masters, they finish as masters, not servants.[11] In the end, they put the local churches, not themselves, out of a job.

You can see why we assign field agents only in the early stages. After a certain point the shift from ministry to movement to monument becomes automatic, and bureaucratization does its own work. Parachurch ministries start with service as their motto and end with it as their epitaph. We cannot have too many such movements. There are a few exceptions to this, but these are extremely rare. "10-10-80" is hardly worth invoking.

Throughout this section I have referred to *reduplication*. But don't forget that copying itself has recently advanced. Therein lies a latter-day parable. Gone is the poor quality and slavish imitation of the carbon copy. In its place the modern copy is highly customized, pseudo-personal and deceptive. (Prayer letters, in some cases, are processed by machines which put the stamps on crookedly to give the appearance of a human touch.) This is the auspicious stage at which Christians have taken to cultural copying.

This concludes my survey of the damage done by modernization to Christian institutions. The damage can be placed in two main categories: first, the general evacuation from the public sphere;

second, the unenviable choice, either to follow the majority and accept the restriction to the private sphere or to side with the minority and attempt to re-enter the public sphere by reduplicating its structures and styles. The Christian plausibility crisis is deepening. There's nothing like two false alternatives for puzzling the mind and demoralizing the spirit.

# MEMORANDUM 9

**SUBJECT:**

## DAMAGE TO ENEMY IDEAS

**FROM:**
DEPUTY DIRECTOR,
CENTRAL SECURITY COUNCIL
**TO:**
DIRECTOR DESIGNATE,
LOS ANGELES BUREAU
**CLASSIFICATION:**
ULTRA SECRET

■

President Ford was once reported to have said, "Whenever I can I always watch the Detroit Tigers on radio." Faux pas apart, radio would be a tame way to tune in to the Electronic Church for the first time. I wish I could have seen your first reactions to some of the more exotic species of *Ecclesia Electronica*. As you say, even *Punch* in its prime couldn't have scripted some of that stuff. Truth here is indeed stranger than fiction. Even satire must humbly bow to reality.

The last time I visited your new post I watched one of their talk shows while changing for dinner. The customary parade of celebrities was passing across the screen, quick-tongued as ever, each one endorsing the Christian gospel with all the sincerity of a toothpaste commercial.

The mood suddenly changed, however, when a Black singer sang an old spiritual in a way which threatened to inject reality into the proceedings. I must have actually stopped dressing for a moment, instinctively alerted to something that might be serious. I needn't have worried. The show's hostess clapped her hands, rolled her eyes heavenward and cooed:

"Fantastic, brother! Fantastic! Christianity is so fantastic, who cares whether or not it's true!"

These little inanities signify nothing, you say. Perhaps not if judged by your academic criteria. But forget for a moment your fastidious preoccupation with intellectual things and what qualifies as *proven* knowledge. We are dealing with people where they are, and where most people are, what *passes* for knowledge is all that matters. Besides, in a day when common religion and cultured religion have parted company, the average talk-show host has immeasurably more influence than the average theologian.

Empty-headed religion of that sort is hardly new or unique to Christianity. (As one EST—Erhard Seminar Training—graduate said recently, "I don't care how much of this is crap. It changed my life.")[1] What is new in the talk-show hostess's remark is the degree to which the Christian faith has lost its intrinsic value and taken on an almost purely instrumental value. It is prized for what it does rather than what it is. No longer does it work because it's true; it's not even true because it works. It works and that's all there is to it.

Such faith is little better than magic, the fine art of manipulating God. I heard a guest on a Christian radio program asked whether he felt there was a lesson to be learned from the life of Eric Liddell in the Oscar-winning film *Chariots of Fire*. "Certainly," he replied. "Blessed are the pure in consciousness for they shall win."

These are excellent illustrations of what modernization has done, not only to Christian institutions but to Christian ideas. I would not, of course, deny that the major damage to Christian ideas has come from other ideas. This is manifestly obvious, and I don't need to dwell on it to a counter-apologist like yourself. Dismissals such as Marx's, counter-explanations such as Freud's, and frontal attacks such as those you have worked on have devastated Christianity. What is left of its former intellectual integrity is as shattered and dazed as the survivor of a nuclear blast.

Having said that, most Christians are untouched, since they live outside the range of an intellectual strike. They've seen the results of such strikes, so they warily avoid entering the danger zone of thinking and debate. This means that there is always a risk for us. Once the fallout has lessened, popular religion may supply the grass roots faith that arms a new movement of resistance.

This is where we have promoted modernization to form the perfect complement to skepticism. Christian ideas have been devastated by other ideas, thanks to skepticism. At the same time, secularizations, privatization and pluralization have provided an atmosphere designed to intensify the problem, deepening the damage caused by intellectual skepticism and extending it into areas where skepticism alone would never reach. Thus, in the age of video space games, Middle-town-wherever will always be closer to Mars than Athens to Jerusalem.

There are three main areas where you can see the impact of modernization on Christian ideas. In each case our objective is to widen the gap between Christian claims and consequences, spiritual rhetoric and social reality, so that Christianity appears neither credible nor plausible. Once this is achieved, we create the situation where, for those who put stock in argument, skepticism leads to the conclusion that Christianity *is* not true; while for those who don't, secularization means that it does not *seem* true anyway.

## Loss of Certainty

The first main point of damage is that Christian ideas have lost their former certainty. Under the impact of the modern world, there has been a definite melting down of faith. Secularization makes the Christian faith seem less real, privatization makes it seem merely a private preference, and pluralization makes it seem just one among many. We are now reaching the point where the content of faith bears an uncanny resemblance to its context. Christian certainty is being diminished and distorted in the process.

Faith has always been pivotal for Christians (as it is not, for example, to Buddhists), so the traditional sense of the certainty of faith has been a key to their survival and their victories—their armor plating against doubt, their steel will in adversity or persecution, their trump card in evangelism, their Archimedean lever with which to move the world.

At the same time, Christian certainty has always been multi-dimensional. It wasn't purely intellectual nor purely spiritual, but a many-stranded combination of spiritual, intellectual, social and emotional threads woven together to form a tough, anchoring assurance.

This multi-stranded character of certainty was its strength. If one or more threads snapped, the others could be counted on to hold the strain until repairs were complete. But given enough carelessness, this many-sidedness could be turned into a weakness, since often people were not sure which strand had gone and which needed repair.

Today's casual attitudes are a tremendous advantage. The vague foreboding that something somewhere has given way is usually quickly dispelled with "Never mind. The rest will hold." The result has been a climate of ignorance and neglect in which we have seen to it that the vital strands have gone for good and those that remain are too weak to stand any real test.

I am not suggesting that certainty has disappeared altogether. It has in some places been replaced openly by doubts or (more respectably) rationalized by notions such as "humility," "ambiguity" or the "confession of triumphalism." These notions serve as a protective theological solution to mask the deepening erosion of convictions once as clear-cut as Gothic carvings.

But in most places certainty has not so much collapsed as changed. Much of the certainty that remains is either a subjective certainty (rooted in subjective experience rather than in objective facts) or a sectarian certainty (rooted in membership in a tight-knit group and lasting only as long as the membership). This, of course, is a fatal change from the traditional Christian certainty of faith.

You can observe this collapse or change at various points. One is where Christians refer to their own faith. In the talk of some liberals certainty is as elusive as the Loch Ness monster. Occasional sightings are reported, but no confirmation is ever possible. Dogma is now dubious and doubt dogmatic. Ambiguity covers everything like a Scottish mist, and in the end a suspicion arises naturally in the minds of others, if not their own: If faith is that ambiguous and that elusive, is there really anything there at all?

Many conservatives, on the other hand, exhibit the kind of certainty which has changed rather than collapsed. They sound as certain, but the source of certainty has shifted. With some the new source is faith in faith itself. Listen to their positive mental attitudes and their possibility thinking. Such faith needs neither facts nor God, only itself. "I'm such an optimist," boasts one such motivational salesman, "I'd go after Moby Dick in a rowboat and take the tartar sauce with me."[2] A sure recipe for selling seminars and books, if not quite what the writer of Hebrews 11 had in mind. Assertiveness has stolen the show from conviction.

With other conservatives the new source of certainty is faith in feeling and experience. Listen to their songs and testimonies, and you'll hear how knowledge words have given way to belief words, which in turn are giving way to feeling words. The faith that remains is beginning to sound like something bordering on an adrenal condition. Its certainty is little better than a "god of the gut," no deeper than its latest experience, no firmer than its current fellowship, no stronger than the findings of the latest opinion poll. (Though, of course, if we are to take the Christian record company seriously, "firm believers" are no longer to be measured by their theology but by their thighs.)

Another place to observe the erosion of certainty is in the changing way Christians identify themselves. Not long ago traditional denominations were glacierlike in their massive historical "givenness"; now they are melting into fast-flowing rivers of choice. Obligations are turning into options; traditions are breaking up and

becoming matters of taste. And as all this happens, ways of identification are changing too. For a Swede to be Lutheran, for example,
was once synonymous with being Swedish, as it was for a Spaniard
to be Catholic. Today, "I am a Lutheran" (or Anglican or Quaker)
melts into "I'm part of the Lutheran tradition" which melts further
and begins to evaporate into "We go to the church around the corner which happens to be Lutheran."

This, by itself, is neither here nor there to us, but notice what it
represents. Christians were once as obstinately attached to their
denominational distinctives as to their fundamental convictions.
Now they're as casual about the latter as the former. Far more than
ecumenical motives are at work. These only serve to divert attention
from the important process of social mixing and doctrinal leveling
through which spiritual content comes to reflect social context. The
glacial mass of traditional orthodoxy has been caught in the great
thaw and is now easily siphoned off to fill the shallow hot tubs of
contemporary religious experience. Human selection, rather than
divine election, is likely to be the ground of Christian certainty
today. Modern believers may not be "chosen," but at least they can
feel they have chosen well.

A final place for you to observe the loss of certainty is in the confusion of theological authorities and ethical applications aggravated
by pluralism. As the disarray spreads, authority is dissolving into
ambiguity and its central question, Who says? is being replaced by
the common answer-cum-anxiety, Who knows?

The trick here is to raise questions which recede in infinite regress
into the mists of doubt. Is there really a biblical message, or is the
Bible only a library of contradictory views? If there were such a message, whose interpretation of it would be right? Even if an interpretation could be agreed on, whose application of it would be the true
one? And so on.

Who knows? can be answered equally either by saying "no one"
or "anyone." The result is a melee of uncertainty and diversity that
borders on chaos. Traditional boundaries between insiders and outsiders, orthodox and heretical, believers and unbelievers are vanish-

ing before their eyes. The rules of the game are unclear and both sides seem confused. (Are the lost really saved, or are the saved merely lost?) Once vital links are systematically being broken (the one between belief and behavior, for example, is kept alive not by Christians, but by the sects).

Mother God? The deity of Jesus a myth? Practicing homosexual ministers? Christian atheism? You raise it. They'll run with it. Almost anything passes for Christian belief these days; almost anything is permitted as Christian behavior. Modern Christian discourse is punctuated only with question marks. Like Sam Goldwyn, it will give you "a definite maybe." A clear answer would spoil everything.

## Loss of Comprehensiveness

The second main point of damage is that Christian ideas have lost their former comprehensiveness. Under the impact of the modern world—particularly of secularization and privatization—there has been a distinct miniaturizing of the faith. Its relevance is restricted to the private sphere, so faith seems real only when people are dealing with private matters. Elsewhere it is silent or only a faintly Christianized echo of the views of others.

The comprehensiveness of faith was once as important to Christians as its certainty. It was the secret of their mustard-seed growth, their restless expansionism. Christian truth, as they saw it, was total. It was meant to cover everything or it meant nothing.

Comprehensiveness was also the sting in their challenge to others. Truth was total; it not only covered everything for those who believed, it challenged everything for those who didn't. Pharaoh, stubborn fool, found that out to his cost. "Let my people go!" said Moses. And what did he mean? Not just the men, and not just for worship, as Pharaoh was willing to grant. But every last person and everything they possessed, right down to the last of the livestock ("Not a hoof must be left behind").[3]

You don't negotiate with spiritual totalitarianism like that. Its creeping comprehensiveness is insatiable. Either you beat it at its own game, or you subvert it from within as we have done.

Many religions would have no problem with such a drastic shrinkage of faith. They're preshrunk anyway, and make no claim to being anything other than privately engaging and socially irrelevant. But Christianity is not like that, any more than Marxism and Islam are. Its claims were once acknowledged as covering all of life. They were a life or death, all or nothing issue. So for the Christian faith to lose its character and capacity as a world view is highly significant. How are the mighty fallen indeed!

This miniaturizing of faith can be seen in trivial incidents or situations of tremendous importance. An illuminating example is the recent *Reader's Digest Bible*, a svelte new version forty per cent slimmer than the more rotund RSV, with fifty per cent shed from around the Old Testament and twenty-five per cent from the New. And why not? Isn't all good preaching a form of abridgment? Isn't the original sixty-six-book edition a trifle long for the busy reader of single-evening condensed classics? It was only a matter of time before the twentieth-century's publishing phenomenon would turn its attention to the world's no. 1 best seller and extract from it "the nub of the matter."

Examine the record of modern digests, and you'll see that abridging and digesting are not what they once were, devices to lead readers to an original which would give them what they really wanted.[4] In today's world the digest is all they want. The abridgment is therefore no longer a bridge to the original. The shadow now overshadows the substance.

The unintended effect of these Holy-but-unwholly Scriptures will be sheer wizardry. What price biblical authority now that the Bible's own stern warning against its being cut down has itself been cut out, and by Christians? What old King Jehoiakim got into trouble for doing with his penknife and brazier, what Martin Luther only contemplated doing with the "right strawy" sections, what they have always attacked liberals for doing with their scholarly scissors and paste, certain Christian conservatives are now doing cheerfully and enthusiastically—and all for the sake of convenience.

There you have it: the triumph of convenience over the canon, of timesaving over truth. The spirit of the modern reader has spoken, and even the divine author is cut down to size, his "essence" distinguished from his "embellishments" like anyone else's. A small step for the *Reader's Digest* but a giant step for conservative Christianity. The very notion of "convenient Christianity" would once have been considered a contradiction in terms. Today, as the reach of faith shrinks, anything else is becoming the preserve of the purist, the fanatic or the crank. Philosophers and theologians can be declared redundant. Today the condensed Bible and the comic-strip version. Tomorrow the complete Scriptures in a single slogan.

Another, more widespread, example is the critical notion of *sin*, a notion central to the Christian view of human nature. Sin once had a collective dimension. It was never a purely individual matter, and among its wider, practical consequences were those which concerned nature and ecology and justice in the economic order.

But what does sin now mean to the average conservative believer? Here is a good litmus test. Whenever you hear an evangelist thundering about specific sins, notice what he names. Nine times out of ten, I'll wager, the sin is a personal one. Adultery? Drunkenness? Drugs? Gambling? Swearing? Those no doubt and more, but all characteristically personal and individualistic. Certain conservatives actually seem obsessed with the idea of sin, but their view of it is so shrunken that they're blind to its original significance.

Another simple test of this miniaturizing process would be to go back to your local Christian bookstore (in L.A., conveniently open on Sunday) and see which books are stocked and which sell best. The topics will be revealing, as will the titles and blurbs. Anything you could dream up for the devotional life will be there. Anything you could desire for the people who watch their feelings as they watch the bathroom scales. Everything for the family, too, and all in the how-to, can-do style pioneered in the secular market.

Where, though, are the books to help the scientist in her discipline, the politician in his decisions, business people in their deals? These are conspicuously absent, and for the Christian to be relevant in public life without them is as hopeless a task as brick

making without straw.

Such examples demonstrate how the silken noose of privatization constricts Christian ideas as well as institutions. In fact, the spiritual content of faith sometimes reflects its social context so closely that it's almost farcical. I passed a church in San Francisco last year, and this was the solemn message on its notice board: "There is a place for duty in work, but not in love." (I confess I couldn't resist stopping to ask if it was a joke and was met with high indignation, which was my answer.) Sociologically, so thoroughly contextual; theologically, so totally contradictory. No wonder divorce is increasing among Christians. With teaching like that, who needs temptation?

At the lowest level, this miniaturizing of faith is one of two impulses behind the proliferation of so-called Jesus junk: bumper stickers, buttons and religious trivia of all kinds. As one lapel button summed it up, "Let your Jesus Button so shine before men that they may see your good graphics and glorify your P.R. man who lives on Long Island." The other impulse (commercialization) I'll bring in next, but you can see here how trivializing is a direct consequence of the loss of comprehensiveness in faith.

My favorite recent example of spiritual "mellowspeak" is a belated birthday card I was shown recently by the Director. The greeting ran: "God's timing is so perfect I cannot feel I'm late/for wishing you God's best is never out of date." What pleasure it would give me to show that to Augustine or John Calvin: The towering doctrine of divine sovereignty reduced to the salable size of a handy excuse for being late.

All these things are quite diverting, and they provide a certain comic relief for the Council, but what matters is the principle and the consequence. One of the major consequences is the way these forces interrelate and aggravate each other. Loss of comprehensiveness in the Christian faith is a boon to civil religion and consumer religion, for instance. Many Christians have so personal a theology and so private a morality that they lack the criteria by which to judge society from a Christian perspective. Their miniaturized faith could never create any friction with the status quo. In fact, it acts like spiritual lubrication for the smooth running of the social system, Christianty's "service with a smile" to culture.

A recently converted vice president of NBC who was interviewed in the *Washington Post* went out of his way to stress that his new Christian outlook would lead to no new moral standards around NBC. "All it does is give me peace of mind in my personal life," he said. "But whether it will affect my programming, it doesn't. It just makes me think clearer, but that just means that I probably think more commercially than I did before."⁵

There's an obsession with anti-Christs today. But it's worth remembering that in most periods (short of the final conflict), one mini-Christ is worth more to us than a legion of anti-Christs.

**Loss of Compelling Power**

The third main point of damage is that Christian ideas have lost their compelling power. Under the impact of the modern world, there has been a growing drive to market the faith.

The general thrust should be obvious to you by now. Social context shapes spiritual content. Why the loss of compelling power? Secularization and privatization. Why the new emphasis on marketing? The nearest modern equivalent to the gospel's dynamic, as they see it, is the sales drive. In other words, the commercialization of Christian institutions has its counterpart in the realm of Christian ideas.

The theoretical symmetry of the Director's plan is so exquisite that it's vital not to miss how it has worked out in practice. But, first, be sure you appreciate the compelling power Christianity once had. It has always had its points of weakness, but that's not the same thing as the condition of settled mediocrity in which it finds itself today.

Only a simpleton could mistake the church today for the entity it once claimed to be. At times in history Christianity has had an almost irresistible attraction. Even more, it was able to command uncoerced obedience. We have never been able to get to the bottom of why this was so. Nor have we adequately explained the mysterious magnetism of the person of Jesus. But judging from the evidence of those drawn into its orbit, the compelling power of the Christian gospel lay in at least three central points: the stark claim to be absolute truth, the strange drawing power of the cross, and the subversive notion of divine wisdom wrapped up in human folly.

Explain such compelling power any way you will. Fortunately, the issue is only academic now, since the original dynamic has been replaced by something far easier to explain and exploit. Let me give you an example. A few years ago I was meeting a contact in Madrid during Holy Week. More out of curiosity than anything else, I kept half an eye on the Catholics' week-long commemoration of the final days of Jesus. Each day had its appropriate services and processions, building up with a heavy accent on suffering and agony to the final Friday. Saturday was dead quiet, and Sunday I expected the usual Easter folderol. But oddly there was almost nothing.

I was intrigued and made a mental note to do some research. Clearly the cultural climate of medieval Spain, untouched by the Reformation, had shaped the church, exaggerating the cross and minimizing the resurrection. I suspect there was some late-medieval operation of cultural subversion similar to our own.

The incident flooded back into my mind a year later, by force of contrast with an Easter special which I viewed during some investigations in California. It was Good Friday, and I steeled myself for the inevitable hour-long meditation on the crucifixion. I needn't have bothered. It may have been Good Friday, but there were no references to blood, pain, suffering or death. The cross was not even mentioned—not once. Instead, there were images of surf pounding on rocks, lilies bursting up through the ground and sun breaking through clouds. The dialog was a kind of Hallmark-card theology, spiritual sentiments supplying wings for human dreams.

I sat through it enchanted. Lotus-land Christianity, California style. Never before had I seen a whole program with so skillful a blend of saccharine spirituality and consumer religion. And on such a day.

Most cases are less developed than this, but the trend is unmistakable. The old compelling power of Christian truth is diminishing, its dynamic taken over by the drive to sell. As we saw earlier with Christian institutions, so here with ideas. The gospel is being modified to become a consumer product; its proclamation is becoming a matter of packaging, and its reception a question of consumer preference; preparation through prayer and study is giving way to market research, and a new type of minister is emerging, half shaman and half salesperson. Doesn't that little L.A. cathedral actually boast of being a "twenty-two acre shopping center for Jesus Christ"?

In a famous description, G. K. Chesterton called America "a nation with the soul of a church."[6] Yes, agreed Alistair Cooke, but also "a nation with the soul of a whorehouse."[7]

Our real triumph, however, is not in the blatant and the bizarre, but in the quiet, ordinary ways this is happening—with the injection of "salespeak" into the testimony over the garden fence or into the small-town sermon which could never hope to draw a television audience. Equally, our real goal is neither the financial scandals of the church nor the bitter jokes about Christian rip-offs. Our goal is simply to add link after link after link to the ever-lengthening chain that shackles the gospel.

What are the practical gains? First, the Christian faith is badly presented. It becomes one product among many, with sales pitches that sound phony at best and crass or fraudulent at worst. You can imagine the panic if a truth in religion law were enacted in the U.S. Who believes propaganda in a Communist country? But then who believes commercials in a capitalist society? Let the church apply marketing attitudes and assumptions uncritically to its communication: Christian truths and experience will be toothpaste-bright and deodorant-fresh, with all the gravity and depth of a catchy jingle and a thirty-second spot.

Second, the Christian convert is badly prepared. Compare the spiritual training and diet of today with the gospel originally offered. Jesus was a forbidding and unsparing leader. He issued an invitation, but made clear his demands. He supplied needs, but required sacrifice. He made promises, but emphasized costs. He was as offensive as he was appealing. No one who chose to follow him could have done so with eyes closed.

Today's spiritual diet, by contrast, has undergone remarkable improvements. It is refined and processed. All the cost, sacrifice and demand are removed. (One of your more progressive, local tele-evangelists has even dropped the tactless word *sinner*.) It's also enriched with a full range of additives from modern psychology. The formidable diet for the great race of faith has now become little more than a quick jag for boosting spiritual blood sugar.

Notice particularly how anything prophetic, controversial or unpopular (but true) is diluted more and more. Stretching further and further for an ever-expanding clientele, Christian salesmen are out-offering everybody, but only by thinning down their truth. Soon its traces will be negligible. What was once the "scandal of the cross" is unrecognizable. It has become not only respectable but all the rage and all the weaker for it—history's encore to the Palm Sunday crowd scene. Jesus again has multitudes who clamor about his kingdom, but few who carry his cross.

Stop for a moment and survey the whole breathtaking scene: the three pressures of modernization, the two strategies for follow-up, the damage to Christian institutions and now the damage to Christian ideas. All this with barely a voice that can break into the church's final sleep.

Undoubtedly you were deeply excited by some of the devastating counter-Christian arguments you were working on before. But in your most ambitious moments did you ever dream there could be a strategy of such sweeping scope and utter simplicity? I salute the Director. The plan's the measure of the man.

# MEMORANDUM 10

**SUBJECT:**

## DAMAGE TO ENEMY INVOLVEMENT
### PART ONE:
### "FOSSILS AND FANATICS"

**FROM:**
DEPUTY DIRECTOR,
CENTRAL SECURITY COUNCIL
**TO:**
DIRECTOR DESIGNATE,
LOS ANGELES BUREAU
**CLASSIFICATION:**
ULTRA SECRET

■

A few years ago I heard a prominent and controversial bishop of the Church of England regaling an audience with a story about the demise of an equally prominent and even more controversial Presbyterian minister and Ulster politician.

The Ulsterman had arrived at the gates of heaven only to be stiffly redirected to "lower regions." Later, in the middle of the night, there was an enormous commotion and banging at the gates.

"Oh, no," St. Peter muttered. "Not that Ulsterman back."

"No," said the gatekeeper, "It's the Devil—asking for political asylum."

The audience greatly enjoyed the joke, and so did I, though not quite for the reason the bishop intended. For behind the jest was a revealing gulf, not between Englishman and Irishman or Anglican and Presbyterian, but between far more serious rivals: conservative and liberal churchmanship.

Nothing better illustrates and introduces the third main area in which we have inflicted serious damage on the church: damage to its involvement in the modern world. All sorts of labels have been attached to the different sides of this gulf—reactionary versus progressive, right wing versus left wing, "fundies" versus "trendies" —but all are a revealing admission that in almost every department of Christianity there is now a bitter division over how to engage the modern world.

Western citizens are aware of their deep divisions in facing the challenge of the Soviet bloc. Are they hawks or doves? Supporters of cold war or of détente? But Christians have generally failed to appreciate how the far greater challenge of modernity has left them just as hopelessly divided. This is fatally compromising their integrity and effectiveness. Ecumenism, as the bishop shows, often stops at home. Thanks to the overwhelming challenge of modernity and the chronically divided Christian response, a credible, united Christianity is no longer possible.

This great polarization is more important to us than such obvious differences as the divisions between denominations. Ecumenism is thought to be a tremendous gain for the church. But if our research findings are accurate, it won't be in the long run. Whatever the gain, it is comparatively trivial. Trends such as secularization and bureaucratization have already shaken the foundations of the once-impregnable denominational walls, so all that the "ecumaniac" is achieving is the dismantling of crumbling masonry.

More importantly, Christians have become so excited about the din and drama of demolition that they haven't noticed the even greater wall of division rising nearby. What is left of old partitions between denominations are as nothing compared with what's dividing different Christian stances toward the modern world.

Civil war has always been the most refined and cruel of wars; the two sides know each other so very well. Similarly, conservative

Christianity and liberal Christianity confront each other implacably, like pope and anti-pope in the medieval world. Each lays claim to the truth and accuses the other of being in error. But each undermines its own claim by failing to see that it feeds on the other and uses the other as one side uses the opposing team in tug of war. If the tension between them were severed, both would fall flat.

The best way to appreciate this polarization is to view it as a continuum stretched between the two poles of extreme conservatism and extreme liberalism.[1] But before we look at this in detail, let me make some preliminary points.

First, remember that our interest in describing it is in broad types and tendencies, not in particular people or schools (although notice that "naming names" has actually increased because of the polarization and has given a lot of mileage to P and D). Reality, of course, is often a little messier and more complicated than the types, which I have deliberately simplified to make a point and to help us discriminate in labeling real cases.

Also, be sure never to allow the question of sincerity to creep into your assessment. Sincerity is one of the strongest drives in the whole movement of polarization. Passionate sincerity fuels the polarization and makes it extreme and bitter (each side, being sincere, regards the other's position as not wholly honest). This becomes useful in allowing us to egg them on and compound the damage. But our first task is to understand the polarization and the extent of the damage it is causing. For that task, the issue of sincerity only muddies the water. Both sides are sincere. The question is in which direction and to what extent?

Finally, notice the distinction between our use of the terms *conservative* and *liberal* and the common religious usage which is restricted to theology. The common usage refers only to the way Christians relate to the modern world *theoretically* (conservatism resisting modern thought and liberalism adapting to it). Our distinctive use is important. In line with our whole operation and its goal of subversion through worldliness, we regard theology as only *one part* of the church's involvement in the modern world. Our categories of conservative and liberal, therefore, cover practical as well as theoretical involvement. We are as much concerned to foster worldliness of institutions, which they seldom consider, as worldliness of ideas, a far more common preoccupation.

This is crucial strategically. Although conservatism defined theologically often coincides with conservatism defined culturally, at other times it may be extremely liberal when defined culturally *and yet not know it because of its lack of a wider category by which to judge itself.* As we shall see of the evangelicals and fundamentalists, this fact allows us to turn Christians who are the most world-denying in theory into those who are the most worldly in practice. Their language masks their lifestyle from themselves.

## THE GREAT POLARIZATION

|  | *Conservative Tendency* | *Liberal Tendency* |
| --- | --- | --- |
| Ideal | Resistance | Relevance |
| Characteristic posture | Defiance | Bargaining |
| Self-image | Speaking (proclamation) | Listening (dialog) |
| Political tendency | Rightward (conserving society) | Leftward (changing society) |
| Common consequence | Containment (stifling the truth) | Compromise (squandering the truth) |
| End result | Sectarianism | Secularism |
| Image of theology presented | Queen of the Sciences in exile | Fashion model |
| Basic problem | How strong are the defenses? | How far should one go? |

Our purpose here is not to consider a comprehensive critique of Christian conservatism and liberalism, but only to analyze the polarization between the conservative and liberal stances toward the modern world. I have jotted down a short outline of the main contrasts between them. As I stressed, this is highly simplified, yet it serves as a rule of thumb with which to make preliminary assessments. Stand back and look at the broad strokes and you will see the real pattern emerge.

In this memo I will examine the conservative tendency, leaving the liberal tendency to the next one. Notice that on either side they are in an invidious position and neither represents a real option. The track record of both extremes makes rather shabby reading. Unable to maintain a balanced third way, Christians have found themselves pulled irresistibly toward one pole or the other.

### Emigrés from a Lost World

Has the clock of history ever been turned back once a broadly based revolution has succeeded? But have the supporters of an *ancien régime* ever ceased to try to turn it back, consigning themselves in the process to the scrap heap of history?

Ask yourself such questions, and you'll see why the Christian conservative is the spiritual *émigré* from a lost world. The *ancien régime* of the spiritual has been overturned in the secular uprising. Like the scattered embers of a once-blazing fire, extinguished in the grate, Christian conservatives smolder and spark in the corners to which they have been flung. Fierce loyalties, long memories, forlorn causes, splintering factions, fading dreams . . . conservatives are refugees from yesterday and show all the marks of the *émigré* mentality.

The easiest way to outline the conservative dilemma is to start from the problems at its core and then to show you the inevitable weaknesses which follow. The first problem is one which has confronted conservatism in every age, not just in the modern world: *It is impossible to be absolutely conservative.* The reason is simply that time does not stand still. So even if an individual or group manages to preserve something from one generation to the next, it may come to have a different meaning (or perhaps no meaning) because it has a different setting.

What is true of communication across languages is also true of communication across generations. An idea or intention can mean the same thing in another tongue or in a different time only if its form is changed when necessary. *Thank you* in English means "thank you" in French only when it is translated to *merci.* In the same way, if there is to be authentic communication from one generation to the next, what is assumed naturally in fluency between languages would have to be paralleled by flexibility between generations.

Here, then, is the conservative dilemma in the face of passing time. Only the eternal does not eternally change. So the less eternal a reality, the more ephemeral it will be. Absolute conservatism is therefore self-defeating; the ideal of changelessness is an illusion. Nothing changes more inevitably than that which refuses to change.

The second problem is peculiar to the modern world. *The central thrust in modernization toward change and choice puts an unprecedented strain on conservatism.* As impossible as absolute conservatism has always been, most premodern cultures naturally bred a high degree of conservatism, sometimes even creating the illusion that time was stationary and society static. In such periods it was change, not conservatism, which needed justifying. For most people conservatism has traditionally been a state of affairs, not a conscious philosophy.

Like a new broom or a revolutionary government, modernization has swept all that away. Gone is the sense of the givenness of things. Choice and change are now the state of affairs. No longer is there anything automatic or assured about tradition, so to be conservative is to be self-consciously defensive. The result is a new nervousness and anger. Genuine conservatism in a fast-changing world is a threatened species, and the aggressiveness with which it defends itself betrays its underlying insecurity. The old assurance has gone for good.

We have therefore forced modern conservatives into a vicious quandary. To defend conservatism well, they must do it in a progressive way; to fight for tradition, they must use weapons which are modern. Like democrats condemned to become illiberal in the process of defending pluralism or humanitarians who become inhuman in defense of humanity, modern conservatives are caught in a double bind. They must sup with the devil, but the long spoon is in short supply. They will resist change to the death, but in the struggle for tradition not a single feature of their familiar world will be left unchanged.

Small wonder field agents find conservative-baiting such good sport. These two core problems are inescapable for conservatism in the modern world, giving it an inherent instability. Traditional conservatism was like a pyramid—massive, solid, stable and almost impossible to overturn. Modern conservatism, by contrast, is like a top—unless it keeps spinning, it falls.

### Driving Them toward the Traps

Once you see its *émigré* status and the problems at its heart, you'll no longer be surprised at the precariousness of conservatism and its proneness to fall into traps. There are seven main pitfalls in its path. Not even a buffoon with boundless energy could succeed in stumbling into all of them, but it's surprisingly easy to drive conservatives from one pitfall to another and thus to weaken their otherwise considerable energy.

The first three pitfalls can be engineered as a result of a conservative impulse to resist modernity by withdrawing from culture (hence "fossils"). The other four are related to the alternative impulse to resist modernity by engaging with culture, although in a distinctly conservative, sometimes belligerent way (hence "fanatics").

*Pitfall one: elimination.* The first pitfall concerns *the vulnerability of extreme conservatism to elimination by force.*[2] This is the rarest pitfall, one that is inoperable in the West today, but I include it for the sake of completeness since it illustrates the dynamics of conservatism so well. The problem for the conservative here is clearly not internal. Quite the opposite. Sensing a menacing degree of corruption or compromise in the wider church or society, a conservative community may determine to be radically different. It may even achieve a level of consistency and purity which contrasts dramatically with the rest of the church.

But if it does this by almost completely disengaging from the surrounding culture, it will achieve its victory at the price of becoming not only dramatically different but totally defenseless. It can then be eliminated by political decision or, as in the past, through mob violence.

This is what happened in Russia around the time of the revolution. Prior to 1917 there were various utopian religious communities which even the Marxists regarded as progressive. But once the Marxists came to power, the story changed. These communities were suddenly seen as reactionary. They were threats, centers of a different way of doing things in a society which could not tolerate such deviance. In order to be consistent, they had become detached; being detached, they had become defenseless. As such they were easily eliminated.

By contrast, the Russian Orthodox Church proved impossible to eliminate. What it lacked in Orthodoxy it made up for in Russianness and became so intertwined with Russian thought and experience that it was ineradicable. Marxists, wishing to eliminate Russian Orthodoxy completely, would have had to break with the best and greatest part of their own past. Pushkin, Dostoevsky, Tolstoy and countless others would have had to be pitched out too.

The pre-Revolutionary story in Russia illustrates the sort of dilemma with which we can confront conservatives. Are they committed to culture? Then they become contaminated and compromised (more Russian than Orthodox, more tares than wheat). Are they different from culture? Then they grow detached and become defenseless. Because they are separate, they become small; and because they are small, they are easily suppressed. Once set apart from the tares, the Russian wheat was harvested with a single swing of the Soviet sickle.

*Pitfall two: ossification.* The second pitfall is also rare today, at least in its more advanced version: *the tendency of extreme conservatism to harden slowly into rigid and inflexible forms, whether of habit or opinion.*[3] Here, once again, the primary problem for the conservative community is not internal. As with the first pitfall, conservatives may be astute in recognizing trends in the wider culture which present a danger, and they may resist them effectively while demonstrating a more consistently Christian alternative.

Nor in this case is the problem external in the sense that there is any threat of outside force. The problem lies instead in the way conservatives achieve their goals. If they achieve and maintain their purity by cutting off contact with the outside world and building a closed world of their own (especially a closed world of the mind), then the lack of challenge and interchange sets off a hardening process.

Communities which do this may be relatively successful in achieving their goals, but only at the expense of stiffening into a permanently defensive posture. Loyalty may still be high and nostalgia will probably run deep. But over the course of time such communities will look like living antiques, Disneyesque reconstructions of a previous age. Inescapable problems will then arise: How do they win new converts? How do they make sense to a new generation? How do they keep their own children?

You can see advanced forms of this in some of the old Amish settlements, or Jewish communities in New York. Milder versions were once commonplace among Christian conservatives of all kinds —that is, until the social earthquake of the sixties jolted many Christian groups out of the sleep of decades and into cultural awareness. Genuine other worldliness is rarely a problem among conservatives today, though separatist tendencies (such as in the Yellow Pages movement and the Christian Schools movement in the U.S.) have allowed us to revive this possibility.

Our simplest tactic to hasten this hardening process has always been to perpetuate any success beyond the point of usefulness. Was Christian abstention from alcohol a striking stance in the gin-sodden world of the eighteenth century? Then harden it into the arbitrary absolute of prohibition and it will do nearly as much havoc to the faith as the original drink. Is this new music something they'll borrow for worship? Then put it in the deep-freeze of tradition, and over the centuries the dances of Calvin's Geneva will become the dirges of the Scottish isles. Is a new way of doing things successful? Then let it be done again and again for ever and ever. Amen.

Remember that what is "best" and "highest" for one generation can be made dreary or deadly for the next. Time has moved on, but the old are stuck and the young are stumbled. There is only one tactic which rivals that of turning the Adversary's absolutes into relatives —turning the Adversary's relatives into absolutes. Achieve this, and ossification sets in at once.

*Pitfall three: domestication.* The third pitfall is less drastic but likely to catch many who sidestep the previous one. It concerns *the tendency of conservatism to become docile in the demonstration of its differences.* On the surface this pitfall resembles the previous one. Once again the problem is not primarily internal; the conservative community or group maintains its distinctiveness successfully. Nor is it external in an obvious way; there is neither the threat of force (as in pitfall one) nor any need to erect a moat and drawbridge of the mind (as in pitfall two).

There is the rub. Without an external threat, the conservative community is neither troubled—nor troubling. It is tolerated, perhaps even applauded and adopted by the world outside, but only so long as it poses no challenge to that world.

I needn't reiterate the pressures which make this pitfall so prevalent today. Privatization in particular is ideal for helping us to produce this effect. Nothing is more domesticated than the "household gods" and the "spiritual playground" faith of the private sphere. Counterfeit forms of faith fit in nicely here too. Ceremonial religion and civil religion, for example, are not only tolerated and applauded, they are actually subsidized. They are as endearing and compliant as a regimental mascot on parade.

This pitfall has become invaluable to us as the desire to create alternatives has grown more fashionable. *Alternative* is the adjective in vogue: alternative communities ... alternative lifestyles ... alternative education ... The list is endless and the idea sounds radical enough. But *alternative* is often merely the term by which small communities parade their distinctiveness and aspire to be a counter-culture rather than the subculture they really are. Rhetoric and reality must part company, of course. Without any effective opposition to the dominant system, conservative communities may be different, but they are also domesticated. They form a bastion against the world, rather than a bridgehead into it.

You can test this social tameness by examining conservative preaching. In particular, listen for any prophetic diagnosis of culture in their sermons and therefore for any sign of tension between their Christian faith and their cultural fortunes. The gospel, conservatives assure themselves, is "the power of God." If preached, they claim, it will be a force for revolutionary change. Like a certain beer, the salt and light are supposed to refresh society where other reforms cannot reach.

But in fact, even when the gospel preached is orthodox and has strong personal impact, it often makes little social impact. The short circuit is this: However orthodox and forceful Christian doctrine is, *if it is preached in a cultural vacuum it will eventually come to rationalize the status quo.*

You can see this effect in the burgeoning Christian rock festivals, in the gap between the explosive terminology of their language and the essential tameness of their lives. Talk of "dangerous discipleship" and "Jesus the true revolutionary" usually amounts to that—talk. It does for some young Christians what drugs do for their secular peers or the portraits of gurus do for devotees in the ashrams. And when the weekend high is over, they all troop tamely back to the same "real world." Even the most revolutionary spiritual principles are quite harmless unless they are consciously brought into tension with social pressures. Therefore, so long as we can keep correct doctrine insulated from cultural diagnosis, our interests are secure.

*Pitfall four: infiltration.*    The fourth pitfall is perhaps my favorite. It has the elements of surprise and irony and can apply equally to conservatives who seek to withdraw and to those who seek to engage more offensively. It concerns *the tendency of conservatism to be so preoccupied with its defense at certain points that it becomes wide open to infiltration at other points.*

Modern conservatism, due to its top-like need to keep on spinning, is a movement in need of a cause. Traditional conservatism was self-assured, with almost everything on its side. Modern conservatism is anxious, with almost everything against it. But give it a cause to concentrate its mind and absorb its energies; its insecurities

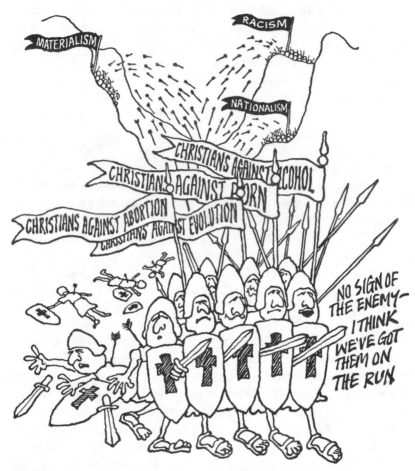

and anxiety will be forgotten in a flash. If they can just rally to where the real battle is, conservatives think, all may yet be saved. With "single-issue" concerns comes single-minded determination.

This determination, you might think, would lead to a heroic performance. Occasionally. But in the long-term struggle it invariably means that, being so well defended at one point, conservatives are carelessly undefended at others. They arm themselves to the teeth at the front door while we slip in at the back.

Even if all-round vigilance were possible in the modern world, it is beyond most people, so the risk of contamination from modernization is always high. But for the conservatives, with their floating anxiety and their constant need for a cause, all-round vigilance is virtually out of the question from the start. Do an end-run around "the cause," and you'll be amazed at the unguarded flank. A current example of this is the preoccupation of American conservatives with secular humanism and their touching blindness to their own secularization. It is true to say that science, technology, politics, wealth and all the great secularizing forces are doing their work behind this generation's back.

This openness to infiltration sometimes results in absurd situations. Certain Christian colleges in the U.S., for example, require a student to sign a pledge not to attend films, while allowing television sets in every dormitory. If you examine this kind of mentality at a deeper level, you will discover how we turn the world-denying into the worldly.

Take a typical fundamentalist. He has a sharper nose than a hunting hound for certain things and can pick up the scent of heresy or modernism a mile away. Yet you won't find anyone more insensible to back-door worldliness of all kinds, which has crept in under his nose. Thus, safely ensconced in their untainted orthodoxy, many conservative Christians have distinguished themselves in this century by a catalog of profane virtues—racism, class-consciousness, materialism and nationalism, to name a few.

As one of them put it to some church leaders in a flash of rare perceptiveness, "If a man is drunk on wine, you'll throw him out. But if he's drunk on money, you'll make him a deacon."

The result we're after is a damning disparity between what the conservatives preach and what they practice. Kipling once remarked about King James I, "He wrote that monarchs were divine, and left a son who proved they weren't." Conservatives today are much the same. Take their support for authority of the Bible, for example. Beliefs about it have rarely been stricter; behavior under it has rarely been looser.

Conservatives claim to be a massive movement of resistance to the culture of today. But as we've seen from their uncritical use of modern methods (such as television and political action committees) and their unquestioning adherence to current values (such as personal peace and prosperity), no one is more modern. Not even the much-despised liberal is more liberal.

*Pitfall five: oscillation.* The fifth pitfall is fascinating. It mostly ensnares those conservatives who attempt to resist the surrounding culture actively. This pitfall concerns *the tendency of conservatism to produce individuals who swing violently from one extreme to another.*[4]

"If you can't beat them, join them" runs the familiar maxim; this pitfall is its unwitting religious equivalent. You must have seen its effects. Yesterday's conservative evangelical suddenly becomes today's theological liberal, yesterday's conservative Catholic today's radical Marxist, yesterday's advocate of "theistic proofs" today's enthusiast for encounter groups. The modern conservative, it seems, is oscillation-prone; and having swung, the rest of life is spent in a series of compulsive attempts to purge a new-found liberal soul of its immature conservative past.

Again it is the permanent precariousness of conservatism in today's world that sets the swing in motion. Conducting a ceaseless defense is intellectually and psychologically demanding, which puts it beyond the capacity of most. This paves the way for the old secret service technique of turning and playing back an enemy's agents, which is called "coat-trailing." We simply apply consistent pressure until the inherent insecurity of extreme conservatism shows through. The sheer attrition of the modern scene is often enough to do it; and then the temptation is to join the other side. As you'll discover, it's not that *even* enthusiasts are defection prone, but that enthusiasts are especially.

This susceptibility reaches its height at times when the icebergs of traditional certainty begin to break up, particularly among those who speak out for the faith. More exposed, they are more aware of the precariousness of their position and therefore tempted to jump.

In the eighteenth century, it was the iceberg of mainstream Protestant orthodoxy which broke up first. Now, following the second Vatican Council it is the Catholics' turn, and the air is blue with the radical rhetoric of ex-priests, former nuns and one-time altar boys scrambling for the safety of new causes. Conservative evangelicalism has been touched by this susceptibility in the past, although sporadically and in random ways. Soon we will make it the focus of a concentrated campaign.

*Pitfall six: assimilation.* The sixth pitfall has snared conservatism for centuries, but now comes in a distinctive modern form. It concerns *the tendency of conservatism to be absorbed into a culture until its Christian identity is lost completely.*[5]

This danger was obviously greater in the past when traditional society and conservative religion were natural allies. When those two joined hands you could barely tell one from the other. Together they had the power to block all processes of change and stifle any channels of dissent, creating a monolithic Christian civilization. In short, the Constantinian solution.

We invariably gained from such a liaison because the fruit of the union was much more the secularization of the church than the sanctification of the culture. This assimilation occurred through the mixing of the bloodlines. Gradually the culture absorbed the church until identification became equation. The church then doubled for culture. Eventually it *was* the culture with almost nothing left over.

You may think this is impossible for us to repeat today. Modern conservatism, after all, now defines itself in terms of its *resistance* to mainstream modern culture. How then can it be assimilated?

The answer is that conservatism can still be assimilated, although less easily, because modern culture is neither uniform nor monolithic. Because of choice and change, diversity is the essence of modern culture. It is therefore quite possible that conservatism may stoutly resist what it perceives as the central drive and danger of the modern world and be oblivious to assimilation at other points. In this sense, the pitfall of assimilation lies in line with the pitfall of infiltration, but just a little further on.

One clear example occurs where conservative religion is used to bolster cultures which are under stress in the modern world (above all in South Africa and Ulster, but to a lesser extent in parts of the United States). Such conservatives are clear about the dangers they are fighting ("Communism," "popery" and "secular humanism," respectively). But the force of their attacks has blinded them to the extent of their assimilation to their own cultures or subcultures. The fact that these cultures at times show an evil face is a bonus to us, but our gains begin much earlier, just as soon as the assimilation begins.

*Pitfall seven: exploitation and/or rejection.* This last pitfall is a logical extension of the sixth, and it is another which has existed for centuries. It concerns *the tendency of conservatism to be exploited because of its usefulness and—sooner or later—to be rejected because of this exploitation.*

Exploitation is merely putting the process of assimilation to work. To get along with the culture, the church must go along with what the culture wants. Becoming one with the culture is what qualifies the church for bonding the culture. Acting as spiritual halo and as social glue are two parts of the same role.

Don't always expect a nation's leaders to exploit Christianity consciously and deliberately. Machiavellianism of that sort is rare, though certainly present today. It happened, for example, in the U.S. presidential elections in 1980, and the attitudes of many conservative Christians made them an obvious target. Confusing Christian principles and conservative politics, romanticizing American history and relying on single-issue politics, they were ripe for the designs of skillful manipulators. But it has been our experience that conservative religion is exploited best when used unconsciously. Each attack on the national or tribal interest it serves is then perceived—and answered—as an attack on the faith itself. The truth and the tribe are one.

This turns conservative Christianity into ideology in its purest religious form; that is, spiritual ideas serving as weapons for social interests. (It also turns the Adversary into judge.)

You can see why we prefer to keep the exploitation unconscious. Christianity turned into ideology involves a self-deception, which is a very different thing from a lie. Both lies and ideologies are concerned with untruth, but while the liar knows he is lying, the ideologist believes he is telling the truth. The ideologist misleads others, but does so unknowingly, a victim of his own propaganda.[6]

Our first gain is this: In deceiving themselves without knowing it, conservatives bring to their ideology a passion of sincerity which even a brazen and experienced liar could never hope to match. Our second gain is more obvious. Ideology is a dirty word today (and far worse to many people than lying). It therefore springs readily to the lips of the critics of conservatism, and when it sinks into the minds of conservatives themselves, it either devastates them or makes them twice as mad as they might have been.

As a counter-apologist, you know that criticism of an opponent's position as "only an ideology" is much abused today. Any argument can be dismissed as ideology—the "moral rhetoric" being distinguished from the "real motives"—once an alternative standard of judgment is imposed. The trouble is that such criticism is itself double-edged. If Communists can accuse capitalists of being victims of their ideology (judged from the Communist perspective), capitalists can return the compliment. The one possibility includes the other. The boomerang can always return.

Christians, however, cannot escape the charge of ideology so easily. Their ideology can be exposed as such without having to go any further than applying their own Christian criteria. Which are the spiritual ideas? Which are the social interests? Is Christianity being exploited, wittingly or unwittingly, in (say) South Africa and Ulster or by the political right in the U.S.?

The answer is manifestly yes. Any serious discussion in which Christian principles were distinguished from cultural practices would reveal that. But is this likely to be recognized? The answer, I'm equally certain, is no. Assimilation, you see, occurs prior to exploitation. Thus, once it is confused with a culture, Christianity can be used by the culture. Exploitation is the price of equation.

In addition, this movement toward assimilation and exploitation builds up powerful pressures which can be channeled toward the rejection of Christianity. "Who among us would be a free thinker," asked Nietzsche, "were it not for the Church?"[7] But is not the same often true today of the African guerilla raging against Christianity-gone-racist? Or of the I.R.A. supporter hardened by Protestantism-turned-intolerant? Or of the cultured agnostic disdaining the crassness of knee-jerk Christian opinions? Christianity-turned-anything is like meat that has turned bad. At its worst, the stench of Christian worldliness is intolerable.

Usually, the more worldly and corrupt Christianity becomes, the stronger is the backlash against it. Yet Christians caught in this backlash often don't examine its significance. (Is this persecution because of faithfulness, or rejection because of worldliness?) Even if they do try to detect worldliness, they tend to measure it solely by the yardstick of Christian origins (judging it as a decline from, or distortion of, the original faith). What they fail to do is measure it also in terms of its outcome, the sort of backlash it is producing.

We can almost always count on this backlash. Some reaction is likely, if in a limited way, even at the preliminary state of assimilation. By the final stages of exploitation, the reaction is virtually inevitable and probably widespread. The trick is to ensure that cultural assimilation is a long slow process of fermentation. With the elapse of enough time it will be impossible for the church to disengage from the culture without being disillusioned itself. Its strength of will and independence of mind will have long since gone.

Look at the collusion of the church and the political right in France after 1789 (the so-called alliance of saber and font), or at Anglican political conservatism in nineteenth-century England—that old jibe about the Church of England being "the Tory party on its knees" (today it's the liberal conscience piously reflecting).[8] How accurate these pictures are doesn't concern us. What matters is that they were *felt* to be the situation, and that is a key to understanding the anti-Christian forces in both periods. At the heart of some of the most militant and effective anti-Christian attacks in history is disappointed faith. Worldly Christianity, especially in its conservative form, brings about its own rejection.

### The Sport of Fools

A word of advice. The bulging files which cover years of operations against the recurring phenomenon of conservatism are all eloquent about one thing: suppress the temptation to indulge in conservative-baiting.

Conservative-baiting, or "fundy-bashing" as it's known in certain circles, is the sport of fools. There is enormous value in the skilled teasing which arouses conservatives to a passion of nostalgia for some lost era. Equally, there are times when a short, sharp prod in the midriff catches conservatism off guard and produces a reaction of maddened and uptight impotence.

Fundy-bashing, however, is different. It says more about the baiter than the baited. It is entirely appropriate when used by the Christian liberal or, better still, by the ex-conservative. Nothing widens the polarization so sharply. But your field agents shouldn't resort to it out of laziness. Far better for them to learn the skills to make the most of the pitfalls.

Consider the record of extreme Christian conservatives over the last two hundred years in light of these seven pitfalls. On the one hand, you can hear the ringing rhetoric, the stirring summons to vigilance and loyalty, the proclamations of authority and manifestoes of concern, the recounting of heroic deeds, the verbal gauntlets thrown at the feet of sundry foes, the muffled tread of millions marching to their meetings.

On the other hand, consider how much these pitfalls account for the reality: the easily eliminated smallness, the calcifying defensiveness, the tame subservience, the carelessly unguarded flank, the pendulum-like swings, the creeping compromises and the flagrant hypocrisies.

Christian conservatives are stumbling unwarily into all the traps laid for them. There is only one thought with which they can comfort themselves. They have fared no worse than their brothers and sisters at the liberal end of the spectrum.

**P.S.** The courier has arrived in the last hour with your response to my two recent memos. Frankly, I am bemused by several of your questions and the general tone of your reply. This time your jousting has rather gone over the top.

It has been my experience that such attitudes in an agent usually indicate either a state of carelessness, a result of the deceiver's contempt for the deceived, or softheadedness which comes from involuntary identification with the target people. Both are signs of a sort of metal fatigue in field agents. But that can hardly be true of you. Nor, to put it mildly, is it worthy of a member of the Council. So I am not sure precisely how to read you.

I expect you to explain yourself therefore in much greater detail. Surely you have not become addicted after all these years to the chronic seminar style (all questions, no conclusions; all discussion, no decision). Nor, I trust, has it anything to do with the Old Fool. There were some raised eyebrows here when you took the initiative to arrange a second and then a third meeting. (Surely you haven't let his cranky jokes get under your skin. I am told that he telegraphs them with a mischievous look in his eye and rolls them around his mouth before delivering them, as if savoring a delicacy.)

What the Director will make of your remarks, I don't know. I should warn you, he's not known for kid gloves when it comes to dealing with hesitations among the higher echelons. He's a grand master of the plausible denial in public, but with our own people his art of the utterly deniable blessing has become most refined. And he's merciless on his own protégés. Only the most ruthlessly tested and proven are trusted. All others are mere agents, strictly there to be handled and run, not known. I look forward to your explanation without delay.

# MEMORANDUM
## 11

**SUBJECT:**

# DAMAGE TO ENEMY INVOLVEMENT
### PART TWO:
### "TRENDIES AND TRAITORS"
**FROM:**
DEPUTY DIRECTOR,
CENTRAL SECURITY COUNCIL
**TO:**
DIRECTOR DESIGNATE,
LOS ANGELES BUREAU
**CLASSIFICATION:**
ULTRA SECRET

■

I was gratified by your prompt response, and I for my part am willing to accept your explanation. As you say, the best covers are never a complete fabrication, merely a plausible extension of the truth. You have played the role of a philosophy don with considerable distinction for many years, so the sort of tenacious questioning which characterized your last memo is perhaps second nature to you by now. Perhaps. It's also true that it's the rare agent who has never had a single flicker of doubt. But don't make a creed of such questions. If you wish to pursue your philosophical reflections or to carry on your offensive against Christianity in obscure, "free thinking" journals, I have greatly misjudged you. Cover or not, our task is too urgent for such indulgence.

The Director, however, would like to question you himself and has ordered a change in plans. Instead of flying direct to Los Angeles at the end of the month, you are to take the Concorde to Washington, D.C., within twenty-four hours of receiving my final memorandum. You will be met at Dulles Airport and taken to a rendezvous with the Director before continuing to L.A. In the meantime the Director wishes it to be clear that under no circumstances are you to meet with or contact the Old Fool again. You have already exceeded your brief. This is straight from the top, so there is no question of altering it. And now let me resume what I was describing before this unfortunate hiccup in our communication.

### Assessment of "Agent Potential"

Just prior to leaving France in the early 1950s, I heard an interview with a former leader of the French resistance. At the insistence of the interviewer he had recounted several of his own daring exploits, and he was asked finally how he explained the heroism and far-sightedness of his men.

"Heroism?" he replied. "No. We weren't heroes. Nor were we particularly far-sighted. We were simply maladjusted enough to be able to see that something was wrong."

I knew this wry, self-deprecating realism all too well. It had been almost impossible to corrupt. While in the Left Bank Bureau I had made it my own personal interest to discover and understand the parallels between the so-called treason of the European intellectuals in relation to the Soviet Union before the war and the same tendency in the church in relation to the modern world. I had a hunch it would open up a new line of thinking for us.

Cynicism and opportunism among European intellectuals had been easy to trade on, but there was always a risk with such easy virtue. They could be exploited by either side and were as likely to create double agents as true partisans. I saw that by far the best conditions for fostering treachery were those which combined idealism (for some cause) and impatience (with one's country or contemporaries). This was what was behind much of the seemingly unexpected infatuation with Moscow of many European intellectuals during the 1930s, whether in Cambridge or in Paris.

I realized that the combination of idealism and impatience was fateful because of the world conditions of that time. Throughout the greater part of the thirties none of the Western democracies showed any sign of readiness to confront the rising power of Hitler and Mussolini; not in Central Europe, not in Abyssinia, not in Spain. Impatient with the complacency of their contemporaries, many intellectuals saw Stalin as the sole leader pledged to resist fascism. They were not aware that their idealism was foolishly naive.

"Treason," charge their critics today. "No," say their friends. "It was not a question of treachery and dishonor, but only of gross misjudgment."

Listen to that discussion for a while, take out the specific names and issues, and you might be listening to a heated argument between the two sides of our great polarization. In many ways the conditions found on the Christian liberal side (the idealism-cum-impatience) and the charges flung from the Christian conservative side (treachery to the faith) bear an uncanny resemblance to the pre-war political alignments. But what I couldn't see in Paris in the fifties was how much the following decade was going to complete the likeness. For if the thirties is the key to understanding the infatuation with Stalin, the decade essential for understanding current Christian infatuation with the modern world is the sixties.

### Seducing the Liberal

Traitors are made, not born. Find a person's Achilles' heel, spot the chink in his armor, feel the old scar, and before long the experienced secret agent will have a candidate for turning. At some point even the professional spy has to come in from the cold; even the illusionless have a last illusion. The ordinary citizen is an easier target still. Dissatisfaction with job prospects . . . over-indulgence in alcohol . . . excessive ambition . . . constantly critical attitude toward the political system . . . fondness for the opposite sex. . . . Factors that make people conducive to recruitment are endless. Nations, classes, flags and loyalties may vary, but there is an extraordinary similarity in the dynamics by which traitors are made.

The particular challenge we faced in exploiting the liberal tendency was this: Where were the liberals open to seduction at a point that would lead them to unfaithfulness? How could we draw them from a flirtation with relevance into a compromising situation with the spirit of modernity? The tactic, of course, was not new. "Apostasy as adultery" was how their own prophet Hosea inveighed against an earlier version of it.

I outlined the dilemma of extreme conservatism in terms of its core problems and their practical consequences. Similarly, let me deal with extreme liberalism by pointing out the steps by which it moves toward a compromising situation and then showing the practical problems this creates for liberal Christianity.

You will remember that *liberal*, as we are using the term, is not a matter of theology only. It is an index of cultural involvement and therefore of the degree of worldliness, so it refers to practice as well as theory and includes institutions as well as ideas. The professing conservative (defined theologically) may therefore be a practicing liberal (defined culturally).

The other point to re-emphasize is that we gain advantage only from the polar extremes. At the point of their respective ideals ("resistance" for the conservative, "relevance" for the liberal), each side is maintaining a principle that is essential to the functioning of faith as a whole. The faithfulness principle (of the conservative) and the flexibility principle (of the liberal) are two sides of the same coin. They are both necessary if Christians are to be simultaneously "in" the world but not "of" it.

We gain only when we isolate and exaggerate the insight of each extreme until it becomes self-defeating. In other words, when conservatism stresses faithfulness without flexibility, it ends by stifling the truth; when liberalism stresses flexibility without faithfulness, it ends by squandering the truth. "Divide and rule" has never been improved upon.

We are playing on a deep tension here as old as Christianity itself.

But in the current situation there are two facts which tilt the balance (or to be more accurate, the imbalance) decisively in our favor. The first is that modern Christians are extraordinarily ignorant about the "etiquette" of engaging in culture, whether in words or deeds.

You know the crisis in conventions which surrounds sexuality today. With no accepted moral etiquette and Christian convictions in between, the distance between shaking hands and sexual relations is shorter than ever before. Indeed, for many people progress from one to the other is as swift and unexpected as the movement in a high-speed elevator with no red lights to indicate the passing floors. They've hardly pressed the button before they've arrived.

Here is the spiritual equivalent of this sexual state of affairs. Modern Christians rarely notice the fateful shift from changing tactics (a matter of adapting to the style and language of the other side) to changing truth (a matter of adopting the substance of the other side's beliefs).

This cluelessness and absence of conventions give us a lot of room in which to operate, for instead of "being all things to all people" in order to "win them to Christ," modern Christians tend to become all things to all people—and then stay there and move in with them. They "spoil the Egyptians," as the Israelites were expressly instructed to do, and then—like the Israelites—create from the spoils a forbidden golden calf.

There is a second fact in our favor. The modern world is overwhelmingly forceful and seductive, so the struggle is unequal. Christians put their toes into the world gingerly and in an instant are out of their depth. They gamble with it cautiously, but lose their shirts as well as their chips. They argue with it passionately, but they might as well be talking to an avalanche. Casual flirting with modernity is an automatic invitation to "becoming involved."

*Step one: assumption.*     The crucial step in the process of seduction is the first one. At the outset, nothing may be further from the liberal's mind than compromise, but like the Chinese journey of a thousand miles, the liberal road to compromise must begin somewhere. This step is taken when some aspect of modern life or thought is entertained as not only significant, and therefore worth acknowledging, but superior to what Christians now know or do, and therefore worth assuming as true.[1]

You can see this step most readily in the area of thought. Do you know of the celebrated theologian who argued that modern people cannot use electric light and radio or call upon medicine in the case of illness and at the same time believe in the New Testament world of spirits and miracles? This is a clear example of the sort of assumption made in the first step. Without realizing it, Christians pass from a description which is proper ("The scientific world view has tended to increase secularism") to a judgment which does not necessarily follow ("The scientific world view makes the New Testament world of spirits and miracles incredible").

Notice how judgments like that dress themselves up in a borrowed authority which really belongs to descriptions. Everyone can see the accuracy of the description; therefore, how can anyone disagree with the authority of the judgment? All we need do then is circulate the judgment with a growing chorus of conviction ("Today it is no longer possible to believe x, y or z . . . "), and it will soon seem self-evident and unquestionable.

What we are sure they will not see (at least at first) is that this leap from description to judgment, or from analysis to assumption, is theologically decisive too. It imports a new source of authority into Christian thinking. Whatever is assumed is then used as the Christian's new yardstick. It is no longer weighed and measured; it weighs and measures all else. It becomes the Christian's criterion rather than the object of his critique. Once the golden calf is in place, it displaces the old altar as the center of the dance.

Only rarely does this happen consciously and deliberately. Most people do it without realizing it. This lack of consciousness is how we can take theological conservatives and turn them into cultural liberals, and how we can move theological liberals toward heresy. The Electronic Church and the New Christian Right are good examples of the former. What stroke of luck, you might ask, could make them distort so many of their own Christian principles? Not luck at all, but logic, is the answer—once you see what they take for granted uncritically. Assumptions about television, for instance, or marketing or patriotism or the place of celebrities in modern society—assumptions all swallowed whole from the surrounding culture.

Talk about swallowing a camel! Ostensible conservatives of that sort can be encouraged to make bitter attacks upon liberals of the theological variety and then buy up the world's value system without a second thought. They labor away at forming their own golden calves while thundering against the golden calves of others. Conservative politics may be the idol rather than secular thought; the Western ideology of development, perhaps, rather than the Marxist ideology of revolution. But the effect is the same. Some aspect of modern experience is assumed uncritically, so that it is made authoritative in practice. In the process the authority of modernity replaces the authority of the Adversary. A defiant "Thus says the Lord" is as passé as a bishop's gaiters.

**Step two: abandonment.** The next step in the seduction follows logically from the first. Everything which does not fit in with the new assumption (made in step one) is either cut out deliberately or slowly abandoned to a limbo of neglect.[2] One infatuated glance at a "new woman" and the "old wife" is seen in a new and unflattering light.

What is involved in this step is not merely a matter of altering tactics, but of altering truth itself. They might excuse their little flirtations by saying they are becoming all things to all people. But consider the one they cite as support for their position. It is true that as he debated on Mars Hill or spoke to the gullible crowd in Lystra, he did not work from his Jewish Scriptures as he did in the synagogues. But this was a tactical device. He reduced the differences between himself and his audience almost to a vanishing point, but only so as to stress his distinctiveness more clearly once they had seen his point.[3]

With the modern Christian, however, the removal or modification of offending assumptions is permanent. It may begin as a question of tactics, but it quickly escalates to a question of truth. Something modern is assumed to be true and proper. Therefore anything in the tradition which is no longer assertable in the face of it must go. Is it embarrassingly unfashionable or just superfluous? In either case, whether summarily dismissed or politely discarded to collect dust in some creedal attic, it has to go.

In effect, what we achieve is anti-revelation, revelation recycled in line with the size and shape of modern assumptions. And the 'dividend for counter-apologetics is reductionism, the voluntary abdication of Christian truth by a thousand qualifications.

You can see it best in the so-called secular theology of the sixties. Had newly adopted assumptions about secularity made transcendence embarrassing and immanence all-important? Then it was time to discard old images and replace old practices, each one buried in its regulation shroud of caricature. God, they said, was not "a grandfather in the sky," but "the ground of being." Prayer was not a matter of "celestial shopping lists," but of meditation.

Liberalism of this sort is refreshing to work with. It is unblushingly frank compared with the closet liberalism of the self-proclaimed conservatives. The conservatives, as we've seen, have lost the objectivity of Christian truth as surely as if they'd abandoned it publicly once and for all. Their Christian message has been cut down to size too. Not dramatically and deliberately as with the proclaimed liberals, but no less decisively. (They have a special place for blessing, prosperity and success. But what of suffering, discipline or simple lifestyles?) In each case the overall movement is inexorable: Something modern is assumed; something traditional must be abandoned.

**Step three: adaptation.**   The third step in the seduction follows as logically from the second as the second from the first. Something new is assumed, something old is abandoned, and everything else is adapted.[4] In other words, what remains of traditional beliefs and practices is altered to fit with the new assumption. The new assumption, after all, has become authoritative. It has entered the mind or the lifestyle like a new boss, and everything must smartly change to suit its preferences and its perspectives. What is not abandoned does not stay the same; it is adapted.

The direction in which adaptations are made depends, of course,

on the new boss. Is he a workaholic? Weekends are likely to be
shorter. Is he tightfisted? Expense accounts are likely to be trimmed.
The same is true of the new assumptions. If the liberals uncritically
assume certain Marxist premises, the adaptation will come out one
way. If they assume premises from existentialism, pantheism, psychotherapy, capitalism or feminism, the results will be as varied and
distinctive as these philosophies.

We take our cue from the assumption, and there is therefore no
surprise in the result. Assumptions produce conclusions as seeds
produce fruit. The only surprise in this part of the Operation is in
the ingenuity with which each assumption is pursued and the solem-
nity with which each conclusion is announced.

Christian beliefs or Christian behavior can equally be adapted,
and we can concentrate on one or the other as strategy dictates. A
simple example is the way traditional words are redefined so that
what was once prohibited is now permitted. Take the case of marriage vows. Conventional marriage, certain Christian liberals say, is
for conventional people. For all others, marriage is conditional.
But what, gasps the conservative, of the clear Christian vow "till
death us do part"?

"Ah," they reply. "You're interpreting it in a wooden, flat-earth
way. It means not only physical death but psychological and emotional death; in other words, the breakdown of an authentic relationship. Divorce is right and proper for a Christian if the marriage
relationship dies. Once you see it that way, in fact, you can say that a
person was never truly married in the first place, so the problems of
divorce and remarriage need never arise."

If the direction of the adaptation depends on the nature of the
assumption, remember that the lengths to which it is taken will depend partly on the assumption and partly on the character of the
adapter. A middle-aged Englishman is likely to be somewhat milder
in manner than a youthful German, and his new theology or new
ethic will probably reflect this.

We must always work particularly to encourage positions which
sound moderate but are radical in implication. Take the current

epidemic of "theologies of the genitive" (a theology of sex, a theology of psychology, a theology of politics and so on). At first sight, nothing looks more admirable from their point of view. Here, they claim, is an attempt to think "Christianly" and develop a Christian perspective on a particular subject.

But thinking "Christianly" is still no more than a mushy notion to many of them. Most Christians are more aware of what it doesn't mean that what it does (what it doesn't mean is often the only topic on which they agree!). As a result, the current rash of theologies of the genitive is largely an outbreak of secularism. Far from being "the Christian mind" on sex or world development or art or whatever, nine times out of ten it is a warmed-over version of the contemporary mind with a Christian rationale tacked on.

As with the second step, this third step cannot be faulted, logically or theologically, if considered on its own. Adaptability, it cannot be denied, is a prerequisite of any cross-cultural communication. Christians were not warned against putting old wine into new wineskins, and Christianity has shown an unrivaled genius for adaptability. Obviously, there is some risk of distortion in any adaptation or translation, but the alternative to taking risks is ossification, which to the liberally minded is a fate worse than death.

The criticism that extreme conservatives fail to do justice to this is true but beside the point. Because here the risk of distortion for liberals is not just possible, it is inevitable, since the alien assumption from which they start is the assumption by which they are shaped. Once an uncritical and un-Christian assumption has been made, any adaptation will be a betrayal by definition.

*Step four: assimilation.* The fourth step in the seduction is the logical culmination of the first three. Something modern is assumed (step one). As a consequence, something traditional is abandoned (step two), and everything else is adapted (step three). If this is exploited well, we can then drive the liberal stance toward the point where the leftover Christian assumptions are not only adapted to but absorbed by the modern ones.[5] This is the fourth step (assimilation), where the original half-truth of liberalism (flexibility) develops into full-blown compromise or worldliness, and Christianity capitulates to some aspect of the culture of its day.

This worldliness is the culmination of the seduction of the liberal just as it is the central goal of our entire Operation. Previous memos are strewn with examples which illustrate this step, especially the various counterfeit religions. Every example simultaneously discredits the power of spiritual conversion and demonstrates the pull of social reversion. Who is impressed by Christian thought or Christian life that has been absorbed by and assimilated into its culture?

In extreme cases we can pull off a degree of assimilation which is not only clear but deliberate, giving the impression of a kind of kamikaze Christianity bent on its own destruction. Take the example of the Marxist Christian Movement founded in France in the 1970s.[6] One of my former agents worked on this, so I have followed it closely (and have recommended him for promotion on the strength on it). When the debates among the members of the Movement became bogged down, they agreed that the point of unity should no longer be Christian commitment but political action (step one reached). This then led to a shift in thinking. No longer were political opinion and action to be viewed as a necessary consequence of Christian commitment (step two reached). Instead, whatever attention was given to Christianity was considered just a part of the wider political commitment (step three reached).

Not surprisingly Christian commitment was eventually eaten up by political commitment. Although the title *Marxist Christians* originally meant Christians (subject) who are Marxists (predicate), the order virtually came to be reversed. The predicate got the best of it, and many Christians withdrew from the Movement, bewildered. Marxism was *obligatoire,* Christianity optional. Marxist theory had seized possession of Christian meaning as effectively as any group of workers taking over a factory floor.

Christians are often blind to this sort of quicksand because of the profusion of Christian words and references in the modern world. Little do they realize that Christianity is like the majestic ruins of an ancient cathedral from which stones are plundered for the construction of countless other buildings. Politicians quarry from its vocabulary, psychiatrists dip into its treasury of practices and symbols, and advertisers mimic the resonance of its acoustics. Each pillager uses just what is convenient. But the decisiveness and authority of any distinctive Christian truth are gone.

There are two main forms of assimilation toward which we should pilot Christians. One is assimilation to *modern ideas,* as Christianity surrenders to an ostensibly superior frame of reference in its pursuit of meaning. The other is assimilation to *modern institutions,* as Christianity surrenders to an ostensibly superior cause or group in its pursuit of belonging.

The clearest example of the first surrender is theological liberalism. Its history is virtually the history of the philosophical and cultural presuppositions of its day. Thus theology follows philosophy as predictably as a tail follows a dog. The average liberal would dispute this, but the best evidence is found in the liberal theologians' criticism of their own predecessors. And what do they criticize? Their predecessors' uncritical adherence to the philosophical and cultural presuppositions of their own day.

Look, for example, at a real liberal's liberal—Harnack. Yet how was his "liberal Protestant Jesus" dismissed? "The Christ that Harnack sees," said one critic, " . . . is only the reflection of a Liberal Protestant face seen at the bottom of a deep well."[7] Modern theology, as another of his critics puts it, "mixes history with everything and ends by being proud of the skill with which it finds its own thoughts."[8]

There you have it. Study today's philosophy, and tomorrow's new theology will come as no surprise. The former Queen of the Sciences has lost her throne and is now earning her living as a fashion model. Scientific positivism? Existentialism? Process philosophy? The dictates and whims of the best European houses determine each season's new lines, although in this case the fashionable designers are usually German rather than French.

The second form of surrender—institutional—is less immediately obvious, but its general dynamic is plain. Christians need to make sense of their world and therefore search for new forms of meaning when traditional certainty is shaken. But they also need to find stability for their lives and therefore search for new forms of belonging when their traditional communities are challenged. Such times provide us with a golden opportunity.

Take the case of young American conservatives, a group we have been liberalizing since the late 1960s and early '70s. Suddenly and rudely awakened by the earthquake of the counter-culture, they rubbed their eyes in disbelief at what they saw of their country and their class. After Vietnam and Watergate, the country for many of them was "Amerika," and their class was the hollow, hypocritical and uncaring "bourgeoisie."

Regardless of whether this was true, it was traumatic. They were not only radicalized, they were suddenly dislocated from their traditions and dispossessed of their emotional and psychological homes. So the search was on for new homes, new forms of belonging, new flags of identification. The results you know well: The passionate pursuit of new causes and the intense identification with new groups (Blacks, women, the Third World, the Left and so on).

Sincere as this search may have been, it was also insecure. It was therefore natural for us to push them into taking positions for psychological and sociological reasons and not only theological ones. Listen to their rhetoric today. A good part of it is an ideology of disaffection, as spiritual ideas now serve as weapons for the social interests of a generation still feeling betrayed by its country and its class.

We have recently launched a similar campaign in Britain. Young Christian conservatives are increasingly embarrassed by their middle-class origins. They are therefore easy to drive toward the harmless delusion that to be anti-establishment is automatically the authentic, "prophetic" stance.

The advantage to us remains the same. In each case, what they have done is exchange an uncritical attachment to one group for an equally uncritical attachment to another. Whether their concern is the comforts of the middle class or any polar opposite is a matter of indifference to us. Our sole concern is that the adherence be uncritical and the assimilation complete.

## Exposing the Liberal

The liberal road toward compromise is rarely taken knowingly. Nor, regrettably, is it always traveled completely. Simple factors like character and time sometimes frustrate our best efforts and keep some Christians from going the whole way. (This is part of the difference between the mild liberal, the "trendy," and the extreme liberal, the "traitor.") But the further liberalism goes, and the more extreme it becomes, the more damaging it is to Christianity.

Our tactics at this point hinge on a carefully executed about-turn. Having seduced extreme liberals into a compromising situation, we suddenly turn and confront them with its consequences. In other words, we drop the slow and deliberate coaxing tactics and switch to a sudden and dramatic confrontation. The result is often little short of shattering. The cruel exposure of extreme liberalism always has repercussions—sometimes on Christian liberals themselves; always on Christian conservatives and on complete outsiders.

Here are some of the main problems for us to exploit in the full-blown liberal stance toward the modern world.

*1. Inconsistency.* The first problem is purely theoretical, so even when it is exposed it will matter only to a minority of observers, although with them it may be crucial. The problem is this: In stark contrast to its claims to be sharp, critical and tough-minded, extreme liberalism is often theoretically inconsistent and quite unself-critical. The reason is that extreme liberals adopt their assumptions in an inconsistent and unself-critical way, although the subsequent steps they take may be logically proper and unquestionable.[9]

How does this happen? In the first place, they fail to make a Christian critique of the assumption in question, so that it is not adopted "Christianly"—it is instead assumed before it is assessed in the light of any Christian belief. The usual passage from description to evaluation or from analysis to assumption is concertina-ed carelessly, as we've seen. The new truth is assumed not only unchristianly (in a narrow sense proper to Christians) but uncritically (in a broader sense common to all thinkers). Finally, the new and unexamined modern assumption is invited to sit in judgment on all previous assumptions.

What liberals don't see until too late is that they have indulged in a sort of favoritism with a hidden double standard, adding insult to injury. Traditional Christian assumptions have been rejected and abandoned, criticized for being products of their time. And by what criteria? By those of a modern assumption, no less a product of its time and assumed in many cases with even less criticism.

I am not suggesting that, if Christians were more rigorous, they would reject all modern assumptions and practices (though doubtless some conservatives might try). Obviously it would be in their interest to accept some and reject others after examining all of them critically and from their Christian perspective. Take Marxism (or any modern belief). The fact that Marxism happens to be one of the languages of the day means that Christians would have to know it and work with it. But to make Christianity Marxist would be both stupid and unnecessary to their cause.

The mistake of the extreme liberal might be called the fallacy of the newer-the-truer. The spirit of modernity seems to have gone to the head of certain extreme Christian liberals, who are now behaving toward it with the adulation of a moonstruck, teen-age groupie. Liberalism is not the tough-minded exercise it sets out to be and, as a result, there are useful repercussions right across the board. The conservative is scandalized, the outsider is amused, and (if he sees what he has done) the liberal is embarrassed. It's only a pity that this inconsistency is seen by so few. Extreme Christian liberalism is the perfect twin to extreme conservatism. The poor thinking is simply in a different place.

**2. Timidity.** The second problem of extreme liberalism again concerns the gap between its promise and its performance. In its early stages, liberalism gives the appearance of relentless honesty, courageous enterprise and daring investigation. Not for the liberal the drawbridge defensiveness of the conservative and the old, worn paths. The modern world is a brave new world, a world for the open-minded to explore and for the initiated to enjoy. Liberalism is bold and spectacular; it knows how to make the news.

So we encourage them to think in the early stages. But study the later stages of liberalism. What of the record beyond the rhetoric? What about the repeated unwillingness to negotiate on Christian terms rather than on those of modernity? Why is it always the faithful who are scandalized and not, even occasionally, the world? Why does the open encounter always seem to end between the other's sheets? Why doesn't modernity run up the white flag . . . just once?

Ask questions like that, and you see that for all its early enthusiasm liberalism is surprisingly timid, remarkably diffident about speaking or acting unless covered by some redeeming "relevance." This relates to your concern about the Operation's being threatened because the cultural tide is changing. To some extent you are correct that many of Christianity's toughest beliefs could be ideas whose time has come. As you say, the notion of Christian love may come perilously close to fulfilling the aspirations of romance and be seen as a bulwark against modern lovelessness and infidelity. Or the Christian concept of evil might be rediscovered as they struggle with the chaos of their times.

You have read the cultural climate well, but your fears are groundless. Consider these brave liberals. Afraid to challenge conventional wisdom at point after point of controversy. Embarrassed to question current optimism about human nature. Ideas whose time has come they discard as opinions whose day is done. Like the well-known "buy high, sell low" of the stock-market victim, they buy into modern ideas at the peak of their influences and sell out on Christian ideas just when modern thinkers are about to rediscover them.

Progress in science has always been made by tackling the most troublesome issues. The very resistance they represent is the best avenue to further knowledge. Through tenacity to creativity, as it were. Christian apologists once followed their own version of this. Face up to those elements in the faith which are obscure or difficult, they said, and you will break through to new understanding. Today's liberals have reversed this. Quick to alter faith as soon as it puzzles or repels anyone, they become susceptible to the special silliness and subservience to fashion of the easily swayed thinker.

Far from being pioneers of change, extreme liberals are remarkably peer conscious. Scrambling to keep up with the cultural and philosophical Joneses, they are fearful above all of being caught in postures which to modern people might look absurd. Just let the modern world look askance at the extreme liberal and, like a chronically nervous strip-poker player, he removes another layer of clothes without even looking at his cards.

*3. Transience.*    A third problem we can expose is the transience of extreme liberalism. Having an up-to-the-minute relevance to one age or group, it automatically risks being irrelevant to another and therefore gives the impression of transience and impermanence.[10]

Relevance in itself is not the problem. As they have correctly deduced, relevance is a legitimate and necessary prerequisite for any communication. To be relevant to a person, any truth must be related to where he or she is. No one would dispute that.

The relevance-seeking of the liberal, however, becomes a problem for two reasons. On the one hand, it has lost touch with its own original Christian assumptions, and on the other hand it has been assimilated wholesale by certain modern assumptions. Relevance of this kind is no more use to them than working hard to catch someone's attention and forgetting what you wanted to say. Or more to the point, it's like being so overpowered by other people's conversation that you express their idea in your words and add nothing to what they believe already.

This basic problem of relevance-cum-subservience has been given an added twist in the modern world, where relevance has become not only hollow but fragile and short-lived. A wider range of choices, a deeper uncertainty of events, a more pressing need for new styles—all this makes for an accelerating turnover of issues, concerns and fads. Nothing tires like a trend or ages faster than a fashion. Today's bold headline is tomorrow's yellowing newsprint.

Thus the relevance-hungry liberals achieve relevance, but the victory is Pyrrhic. It is precisely as they win that they lose. As they become relevant to one group or movement, they become irrelevant to another and find themselves rudely dismissed. Far from being in the avant-garde, Christian liberals trot smartly behind the times. Far from being genuinely new or radical, they catch up and announce their discoveries breathlessly, only to see the vanguard disappearing down the road on the trail of a different pursuit.

"He who marries the spirit of an age," said Dean Inge, "soon finds himself a widower." *Trendier than thou* has eclipsed *holier than thou,* and our gain is evident. The pursuit of relevance in the liberal mode is a cast-iron guarantee that, by definition, the church will always lag behind the world and run at the rear of the pack. The world changes its agenda constantly, and the church goes around in circles.

**4. Destructiveness.**   The fourth problem of extreme liberalism is the most practical and decisive, and for our purposes it is the jackpot. Liberalism becomes destructive for the church in a number of key areas. Each of these areas is important in itself, but the combined effect is devastating, attacking the church like a cancer which spreads successively through all the vital organs.

The first area where liberalism is destructive is where *it loses the distinctive content of the Christian faith.* Of course, Christianity has had many expressions over the centuries; its history has been one of new spiritual movements, theological developments, social adaptations and institutional experiments. Regrettably, many of these expressions of the faith have stuck to Christian rules and remained within bounds, so they have been little use to us. But what worldliness we did achieve in the past was hard-won compared with the easy success made possible by liberalism today.

Today's liberalism collaborates willingly. It seems surrender-prone at heart. Absolutely nothing in traditional belief or practice is sacrosanct. There are no higher or more central truths by which the church will stand or fall. Heresy is orthodoxy; skepticism is faith; unbelief teaches and ministers. Everything is negotiable, the kernel as well as the husk, the baby as well as the bath water. Indeed, you might wonder whether any conceivable crisis of faith is still possible for liberalism. Like someone intent on hara-kiri, nothing short of disembowelment is enough.

The second area where liberalism is destructive is where *it creates a gap between ordinary believers and the intellectual and bureaucratic elite in the churches.* This is no accident. To adapt George Orwell, we might say that it is a strange fact, but unquestionably true, that almost any extreme liberal would feel more ashamed of affirming the Apostles' Creed than of refusing to give to charity. The result is that, just as the pitfall of "oscillation" sometimes propels a conservative toward the liberal extreme, so the extremes of liberalism make ordinary believers so confused and angry that they harden into the concrete mentalities of extreme conservatism.

After all, what are ordinary believers to make of these cognitive gymnastics? These much-heralded new theologies? These situational personal morals? These prophetically radical political stances? Aren't these suspiciously like the beliefs and practices they were always taught to identify as sin and unbelief? And so there starts to be grumbling in the camp. Why send missionaries overseas if unbelief is alive and well in the pulpit? Why put money in the collection plate if it goes to self-professed enemies of the church?

As the dismay and defections mount, a strange fact becomes apparent. While in most institutions the leadership is more committed to the goals of the institution than are the rank and file, the opposite is true of the church. Its members are more loyal than its leaders.

The Christian elite are getting themselves into a position where it is almost impossible for ordinary believers either to understand them or to take them seriously. Take the case of extreme liberals arguing in print the opposite of what they assume at the Communion table. This is how the Christian elite can pursue ecumenism and open a gap behind it wider than any it bridges. With leaders like that, small wonder that as convictions fly out of the window, congregations flow out of the door.

The third area where liberalism is destructive is where *it is inher-*

*ently weak in attracting outsiders.* Yet another superb irony. The very raison d'etre of liberalism began with their man Schleiermacher's concern for the "cultured despisers" of the gospel. What then has this concern achieved after two hundred years? Where are the cultured despisers who have been culturally disarmed? The intellectual prodigals brought back from the far country of doubt and despair?

Confront liberals with such questions and their discomfiture is plain. Things seem to have changed a little since those early days. The item is no longer on the agenda. The cultured despisers most on their minds now are themselves. Few doubters are more doubtful than the extremely liberal believer.

And what does the record show? It should be embarrassingly clear to them that of those intellectuals and artists who have been converted in the last two centuries the overwhelming majority have been attracted to traditional and more conservative churches. Take T. S. Eliot, W. H. Auden, C. S. Lewis, Dorothy Sayers or the Old Fool himself. Why they took the road to religion will always remain a mystery, but they had undeniably keen minds and a certain intestinal fortitude. They took their faith neat and couldn't stomach the tepid and diluted offerings of liberalism.

Who knows? Perhaps liberalism faces one further crisis of faith after all—its unquestioned belief in the dogma that "modern man" finds traditional belief incredible.

To make matters worse for them, there is evidence that when intellectuals reject liberal Christianity they do so for a reason basic to its liberalism: When the most radical liberal revisions are complete, the result is little different from what the outsider believed anyway. "At that point," as one atheist puts it succinctly, "the creed becomes a way of saying what the infidel next door believes too."[11] Thus, since extreme liberalism ends in surrender, its carefully worded, latest statements have an oddly familiar ring. The secular thinker can always respond in Oscar Wilde's words, "I not only follow you, I precede you."

From the perspective of the outsider, the liberal effort is wasted. The very extremity of liberalism only confirms the skeptic's criticism of the faith. As one of the enemy agents sympathizes, "Why should one buy psychotherapy or radical liberalism in a 'Christian' package, when the same commodities are available under purely secular and for that very reason even more modernistic labels?"[12]

After seeing the report of a recent Christian commission on morality, an atheist wrote, "It is now announcing to the secular world, as though by way of a discovery, what the secular world has been announcing to it for a rather long time."[13] Agnostic intellectuals may respect the liberal stand of extreme liberals, but rarely do they take their Christianity seriously. One secular thinker even goes so far as to call them "kissing Judases" (following Kierkegaard). "To be sure," he adds, "it is not literally with a kiss that Christ is betrayed in the present age: today one betrays with an interpretation."[14]

The fourth area where liberalism is destructive is where *it actually undercuts itself.* This is the best effect of all. Just as absolute conservatism is a contradiction in terms, so absolute liberalism defeats itself. When taken undiluted, it kills. No one could find a surer method for spiritual suicide.

You don't need to look further than the startled, even disbelieving, responses which extreme liberalism has drawn either from within the church or outside. "Symptoms of the very disease for which they profess to be the cure," comments one non-Christian of liberals.[15] A "self-destructive outburst" is the surprised and amused reaction of other non-Christians.[16] And from within the church? The comments of one intelligence expert are enough. Extreme liberalism, he says, becomes a *reductio ad absurdum*, a "theological self-disembowelment," a "self-liquidation ... undertaken with an enthusiasm which verges on the bizarre."[17] To any outsider, the practical results might well appear "a bizarre manifestation of intellectual derangement or institutional suicide."[18]

Evidence to substantiate this is easy to find. A well-known example is the current realization that conservative churches are growing while liberal churches are barely holding their own, if not declining. But take a lesser-known case, the collapse of the Student Christian Movement on many British campuses after the 1960s.

There, if ever, was a clear case of organizational suicide, for the
S.C.M. fell victim to its own pathological open-mindedness. As research has shown, it began as a beacon of liberal virtues. No group
could have been more open, more humble, more eager to engage in
dialog, more zealous to build bridges to all and sundry. And bridges
were built—to Marxism, pacifism, psychoanalysis, alternative communities, group therapy.

But then what happened? The conversations in the dialog and
the traffic on the bridges became one-way. S.C.M. members flowed
across to become bona fide activists or to join bona fide communes.
Their original S.C.M. groups did not survive, and there was no distinctive Christian reason why they should. Their minds had become
so open that they were vacant. Diluted beliefs led to defections and
betrayals.

**Beyond Treason**
Defector, collaborator, fellow traveler, fifth columnist, quisling,
turncoat, traitor . . . little throwaway words, but like small fuses they
run off to powerful incendiary passions that are capable of blowing
apart people and nations and faiths. Our interest, of course, is not in
concentrating our effort more on the conservative or the liberal
side, except as a short-term tactic to divide them further. Our real
objective is to push the liberals and eventually the whole church to
a state beyond treachery, to a point at which *treason itself loses its*
*meaning.*

Treason, like heresy, is always an achievement which marks an
important milestone in manipulation. Significant individuals or
groups in a victimized nation come to re-evaluate their country's
traditional foreign-policy interests so that the policies come to be
aligned with those of the aggressor. Whether they do so out of conviction or are merely rationalizing (or even bought) is neither here
nor there. Subversion is well under way, and that is what matters.

The final destination, however, is a state beyond treason. When
the individuals or groups in question are so committed to accepting
outside influence and help that they reject the criteria by which

*loyalty* and *treachery* have traditionally been defined, then treason itself loses meaning. And when treason loses meaning, no nation can effectively resist an outside aggressor for long.

The symmetry with heresy is perfect. Do you see where we are with the extremely liberal wing of the church? "Their trade is treachery" might well apply to the sell-out of full-blown liberalism during the first stage of subversion. But we've gone far beyond that now. With no loyalty to define treachery and no orthodoxy to define heresy, full-blown Christian liberals are reaching a state beyond treason that presages the capitulation of the church itself.

Having crossed frontiers so often that they have forgotten where they are, die-hard liberals have become like the agents-turned-double-agents of the espionage world—the gray no-men of the twilight no-man's land. They are the stateless ones of the modern intellectual world, the wandering Jews of the realm of the spirit, nomads in a desert of abandoned faith. Winning a single Judas was one thing; being able to rely on a counter-elite of Judases is quite another.

# MEMORANDUM 12

**SUBJECT:**

# THE LAST CHRISTIAN
# IN THE MODERN WORLD

**FROM:**
DEPUTY DIRECTOR,
CENTRAL SECURITY COUNCIL
**TO:**
DIRECTOR DESIGNATE,
LOS ANGELES BUREAU
**CLASSIFICATION:**
ULTRA SECRET

■

This is the last of my memoranda briefing you on Operation Grave-digger. It is not so much a separate memo as a short tailpiece to the others (the twelfth of my "counter-apostles," as my secretary has dubbed them). I am also enclosing your ticket for Saturday's flight to Washington, D.C., via BA 189. As you can see, check-in is only forty-five minutes before the 11:45 departure, unless you wish to indulge in the perks of the Concorde lounge.

As things stand now, I am planning to be with the Director when he interviews you on your arrival in D.C. I trust I have adequately impressed on you the need to be concise and convincing. He regards philosophical digressions as a waste of time and a sign of uncertainty. Both are cardinal sins in his book and could become irremediable blots in yours.

You did not know this, but before being assigned to Los Angeles you were slated to succeed the retiring Bureau chief in Moscow. The suggestion that you should go to Los Angeles instead was mine. I have watched your progress closely and have an interest in your success. If you have kept up with the activity of the Moscow Bureau, you'll know that recently they've contributed little else than *The Atheist's Pocket Dictionary,* published a year or two ago. I have saved your career from a cul de sac, so I expect you to clear the shadow hanging over you, to get yourself out of the imbroglio this weekend and to produce results in L.A.

## Beware Third Ways

You asked me which was the most significant of the three major areas of damage (damage to the church's institutions, ideas or involvement in the world). I would have to say the last one. Nothing else so calls into question the integrity of Christian truth as well as its capacity to respond to the modern challenge. And the added advantage for us is that it is the area where Christians are least aware of the damage being done.

In the great polarization, each extreme is acutely aware of the danger of the other, as I've said. Conservatives feed on the perils of liberalism, just as liberals grow more dogmatically liberal to avoid the horrors of conservatism. But seldom do they consider the problem as a whole; and it is unimaginable that they should mobilize to work for a solution that overcomes the polarization altogether.

The only thing we need to watch, as always, is recklessness. The worst thing that could happen is this: The increasingly apparent weakness and captivity of the church might jolt Christians into seeing the force of the extremes and then spur a movement to recover a coherent and balanced, ruthlessly biblical "third way." If you like, a resistance movement content to be neither *émigrés* nor collaborators. The time for such a movement is ripe, for if the sixties illustrated the absurdities of extreme liberalism, the late seventies has done the same for extreme conservatism. The cry "A plague on both your houses!" would be a fitting tribute to our work, but it could also spell trouble for us. Nostalgia for a golden age is harmless; the desire for a golden mean is not.

Fortunately, any movement is unlikely to develop momentum, and the odds against achieving such a third way are impossibly long. For one thing, the whole notion is permeated with the suggestion of compromise, as if balance were a congenital English weakness for refusing to take sides or to go to extremes. More importantly, the forces within the great polarization are so strong that no movement could hope to hold the middle ground for long.

Having said that, if my sources are right, I do expect to see such an attempt soon. It will most probably come from chastened conservatives, such as certain evangelical and Catholic groups, though perhaps with the support of certain more moderate liberals too. We are ready for this. The Council has made no formal decision yet, but in my judgment we would be wise to adopt the following approach.

On the one hand, we should do everything possible to *prevent the chastened conservatives from escaping the constrictions of modernity*. Since the 1960s, the general movement of conservatives has been out of the closet and into the culture, sometimes even out of the backwoods and into the limelight. This should be heady enough for them, without any radical talk of a third way. ("It is charming to totter into vogue," as Horace Walpole put it.) Their new cultural involvement should blind them to the constrictions of modernity: secularization, pluralization and privatization. Unless it breaks these chains, conservative Christianity will never be more than a harmless, if popular, folk religion.

On the other hand, if they succeed in escaping the constrictions, we should do everything possible to *push the chastened conservatives to refuel the liberal cycle*. If they were harmless while inside the cultural closet or out in the intellectual backwoods, we can make them harmless again by pushing them to the opposite extreme and launching them on the liberal merry-go-round. This is not as difficult as it sounds. Emerging from the stuffy darkness of their ghettoes, conservatives are now basking in the light of cultural attention. Once a generation or two behind the times, they are making up for lost time with zest and abandon. Nothing is now further from their minds than their old, instinctive fear of worldliness. So who better than these new conservatives to refuel the cycle of the old liberals?

**The Last Christian in the Modern World**
When you arrive in California you will begin receiving detailed instructions from the Council on how Los Angeles is to proceed in this final stage of the Operation. But before meeting the Director on Saturday make sure that your grasp of the Operation is comprehensive as well as meticulous. You will find few things so conducive to clear thinking as the view from a Concorde at sixty thousand feet.

In closing, let me describe to you an aspect of the Director's plan which has always fascinated me: the cultivation of the last Christian in the modern world.

This is not literal, of course. Nothing could be further from our plans than a pogrom. As I've stressed, even so important a tactic as secularization is not directed at faith's disappearing, but its changing. You may remember the secret revolutionary cell in Dostoevsky's *The Possessed*. The aim of this group was systematically to destroy society and the fabric which held it together, with the object of throwing everyone into a state of hopeless confusion and despair mixed with an intense yearning for self-preservation and some guiding ideal. Then it could suddenly seize power.

The final stages of our Operation will be remarkably similar. We are working slowly and steadily to demoralize the church and discredit it in the eyes of the watching world. In particular, to see that the church becomes sick, gross, bizarre and hypocritical in various ways, but always so that its confusion and compromise are matched by at least one thing—its complacency.

You can see how far we've advanced. At the turn of the century, even after a hundred fifty years of the Operation, most of the odds still seemed stacked against us. It appeared no accident that the rich and powerful nations were Christian, while the non-Christian ones were poor and seemingly backward, their religion dormant and their cultures moribund.

Christianity seemed synonymous with civilization; zealous evangelizing and high-minded civilizing went hand in hand. No one had heard of Lenin, Stalin, Hitler, Mao, let alone dreamed of an Islamic resurgence or an East Asian economic miracle. That the coming century would have been a turbulent one of such horror and violence and that so many of the worst crimes should have come from "Christian nations" would have been unthinkable.

Today, by contrast, the odds are stacked against the church. In terms of the burden of her past, she will soon, like the builders of Babel, be buried under the rubble of her own towering achievements; while in terms of the seductions of today, she is about to be drowned, Narcissus-like, in the deceptions created by her own undisciplined brilliance, wealth and enterprise.

The great survivor of the centuries, the proud tamer of empires, nations, faiths and ideologies, is being savaged by modernity. Soon all that will remain is a little philosophy, a little morality, a little architecture and a little experience.

The Director now regards American Christianity as the decisive arena for the closing stage of the Operation, which he views as a movement with three phases leading toward the denouement.

First, comes the *push* phase, well underway at the moment. American Christians have been forced to face the extent, not of their captivity, but of their impotence. Now, in a desperate push for power, many of them are attempting to seize such power levers as political action, legislation, education and the mass media. But, since the drive for power is born of social impotence rather than spiritual authority, the final result will be compromise and disillusionment. Christians in this first phase are falling for the delusion of power without authority.

As this phase peaks, it leads naturally to the second. This is the *pull* phase, when Christians will be jerked back and reminded of their need, not for power, but for principles and purity, even at the expense of powerlessness. The gears will be suddenly thrown into reverse, and the drive for power will be switched to a call for "disentanglement from the powers." Power without authority, power born of the shame of impotence, will be renounced for the sake of authority without power, powerlessness born of the shame of impurity. But—and here the calculations have been precise—since this will happen when traditional theologies of cultural transformation (such as the Reformed) are in evident decline, leadership in this phase will pass to theologies stressing prophetic detachment, not constructive involvement.

By the end of the second phase the effect will be vicious. Uncritical pietism will have been succeeded by hypercritical separatism. Being essentially worldly, the former is rapidly fueling reactions to itself that will put new life into flagging secular ideologies; being essentially otherworldly, the latter will tend to withdraw from society and create a vacuum which these ideologies will speedily fill. And the last state of the house of American culture will be worse than the first.

Then comes the third phase, *press,* the Director's own signature to the finale. Individual Christians of integrity will view these hapless alternatives and be incited to frustration, anger or grief. There will then be a fleeting moment when they feel so isolated in their inner judgments that they wonder if they are the last Christian left. This movement from insight to isolation does not last long, and when the emotion drains away it leaves only a sense of shame for the presumption of such a judgment.

This is how we pick off the caring one by one. Ashamed by their secret arrogance, they sink back disheartened to the general level, their spirits sagging and their vision dimmed. Ashamed to be different, they assent to be demoralized. They thus produce the state they fear. The "last Christian" comes one person closer each time.

All this, of course, is the minority dilemma (the dilemma of the concerned) and the American version at that. The way we deal with the complacent majority is far easier: We simply keep them asleep. As I said in the first memo, the only thing that matches my satisfaction at the church's deepening captivity is my amazement at Christian credulity. I sometimes wonder if they think they are immortal.

Or if they consider themselves exempt from the normal rules of human experience and spiritual life. They believe their faith can give birth to renewal. Do they not believe it can also die?

They remind me of a tale of Nasreddin Hodja, the celebrated Turkish holy man. He once borrowed a large cauldron from his neighbor. When some time had passed, he placed a small metal coffee can in it and took it back to its owner.

"What is that?" said the latter, pointing to the small can.

"Oh," said the Hodja, "Your cauldron gave birth to that while it was in my possession."

The neighbor was delighted and took both the cauldron and the coffee can. Some days later, the Hodja again asked his neighbor to lend him his cauldron, which he did. This time a few weeks passed, and when the neighbor felt he could do without his cauldron no longer, he went to the Hodja and asked him to return it.

"I cannot," replied the Hodja. "Your cauldron has died."

"Died?" cried the neighbor. "How can a cauldron die?"

"Where is the difficulty?" said the Hodja. "You were glad to believe it could give birth. Why will you not believe it can die?"

When the time comes, even the Adversary will put it no more clearly than that. Until then, the Operation proceeds. Let them dig on.

# Afterword:
# On Remembering the Third Fool and the
# Devil's Mousetrap

To be candid, no part of my involvement in the publication of these papers has put me in more of a quandary than writing this afterword. Yet my source was adamant. The papers by themselves could lead to a bleak and pessimistic conclusion, which would be the exact opposite of what he intended. Nor would they give more than the slenderest of clues as to why he himself was defecting to the Christian side.

On the other hand, he was emphatic that nothing could serve the papers worse than a fairy-tale ending. Pious romanticism or a simple reiteration of truisms would gloss over the stark problems and convince no one. Smart secular people, he said, do not like books which preach at the end. And those orthodox believers who do not like having their brains teased could use the afterword to take refuge from the burden of the papers.

My dilemma, then, has been to do justice to his desire and at the same time to make sense of what was no more than a lightning explanation of the thinking behind his disillusionment and defection. A quarter of an hour was all too brief for him to give me more than the ends of some threads of thought which I have since been unraveling on my own. If and when his own full account of the defection is published, it may be judged whether my grasp of his points has been developed in the right direction.

**The Turner Turned**

It appears that for some time, even before his nomination as Director of the L.A. Bureau, he had been growing disillusioned with the direction of their struggle. It was going to become, as he put it, a Vietnam war of the spirit, a war they could not win but would not dare abandon. His sense of uneasiness had only seemed to increase as each post-Christian alternative proved more dreary and insubstantial than the Christian position it had been intended to replace. Curiously, these doubts were magnified even further as the Gravedigger memoranda started to flow across his desk, especially as he turned from the chess playing of counter-apologetics to the realities of cultural subversion.

The switch itself had been easy enough, and the prospect of California was not uninviting. What unsettled him was something else. The Deputy Director had been half right in his barb about the ivory tower. But the ivory tower for my source was not the academic world; rather it was his confidence in the viability of secularism.

He found himself caught uncomfortably between the opposing stratagems of an elitist secularism and an exotic spirituality; the one unpopular with most people, the other unpalatable to him. His mind was plagued by an old saying which kept returning to him like an unthinkable thought, that while nothing is worse than bad religion, nothing is more necessary than true religion. Were even his best agents merely "cheerless atheists, religious fanatics turned inside out"?[1]

All this cast a different light on the Operation itself. It pivoted on a monumental irony, yet as he had once written to the Deputy Director, irony was not a monopoly of either side. Only the side with the ultimate truth could be sure of having the last laugh.

In the end it was laughter which triggered the breakthrough for him. The moment came when he was interviewing the Old Fool (as they refer to the distinguished writer) for the last time. The latter, sharing what he described as his "operational orders" as a convert late in life, had added a maxim of his own: "Love laughter, which sounds loudly as heaven's gates swing open, and dies away as they shut."[2]

Nietzsche had raised the right question (Who is wise enough for this moment in history?), my source said, but Nietzsche had no answer. As he talked and laughed with the Old Fool, he suddenly saw an alternative to the impossible ideal of the Superman and the all-too possible madman. The way out was through the fool. A note of exhilaration entered his voice that night in Radcliffe Square. "The fool!" he exclaimed. "The answer is the fool. We'd been dealing all along with the *third* fool."

Talk of a third fool was Greek to me, and my source barely enlarged on it, apart from stating the kernel of what it meant to him and telling me where to follow it up. If I have developed it correctly, the gist of his point was this. The first fool is the *fool proper*, the person who by heaven's standards is called a fool and deserves to be. This is the fool who litters history with the vast carelessness of his moral stupidity, who appears frequently in the pages of the Old Testament and who fills the passenger list of Sebastian Brant's great satire of medieval folly, *The Ship of Fools*. This, he said, is the sort of fool the Christian worldling becomes.

The second fool is the *fool bearer*, the person who is ridiculed but resilient, the comic butt who gets slapped but is none the worse for the slapping. In Christian terms, the second fool is the one who is called a fool by the world, but who neither deserves it nor is destroyed by it. What is important, since it links the second fool to the third, is the secret of this resilience. The quicksilver spirit of the second fool springs from the Christian vision of the discrepancy between the apparent and the real, between the way things are and the way things will be. Knowing this discrepancy, the fool bearer is always able to bounce back, and his laughter is neither bitter nor escapist but an expression of faith. It is the kind of laughter which absorbs pain and adversity and, seeing beyond them, in situations of despair becomes a sign of hope.

The second fool is the "fool for Christ." From the apostle Paul to Francis of Assisi and Clare to Thomas à Kempis down to the despised and persecuted believers of the twentieth century, the great tradition of "fools for Christ" has never lacked an heir and will play its part here too. As Reinhold Schneider wrote from his experience as a courageous poet in the Christian resistance movement in the thirties, "Anyone who goes against the spirit of the age in the name of the Lord, must expect that spirit to take its revenge."[3] Wherever the gospel has been in contention they have stood like lightning rods in the storm. But seizing the initiative and turning the tables were never meant to be their brief.

Table-turning is the forte of the third fool. This is the person who appears a fool but is actually the *fool maker*, the one who in being ridiculous reveals. The third fool is the jester; building up expectations in one direction, he shatters them with his punch line, reversing the original meaning and revealing an entirely different one. Masquerading perhaps as the comic butt, he turns the tables on the tyranny of names and labels and strikes subversively for freedom and for truth. From the apostle Paul (again) to Nicholas of Cusa to Erasmus to G. K. Chesterton, this strain of brilliant Christian fooling has never quite died out, yet it has never been as common as the first fool nor as honored as the second.

"Who then is wise enough for this moment in history?" my source said, gripping my arm. "The one who has always been wise enough to play the fool. For when the wise are foolish, the wealthy poor and the godly worldly, it takes a special folly to subvert such foolishness, a special wit to teach true wisdom." When the significance of this dawned on him, he said, it was as if he had been caught off guard and catapulted toward the one conclusion he had not expected: All along it had been he who had played the fool while the fool maker had been "the Adversary."

It had been one thing to realize, he continued, that the last laugh and the ultimate truth belonged together. The inner story of his life was evidence for this. Chinese box after Chinese box, Russian doll after Russian doll, had been opened and had been discarded as he searched for the one that would not open, the kernel beneath the husks.

But suddenly he came face to face with truth itself, and it was calling into question every lie and half-truth short of itself—and doing so, not just abstractly and in general, but concretely, specifically *and in person.*

It was this which cornered him and forced him to the turn-around. He who had been skilled at turning others had been turned himself. That night in Radcliffe Square he talked about the prophetic fool making of the divine subversive. He talked about conversion as the supreme turn-around. He talked about the Incarnation as history's greatest double-entendre. And then he was gone.

**Fool's-Eye View**

Precisely how this helps us face the challenge of the Gravedigger papers, he did not have time to elaborate. So I have struggled with what to say and to say quickly as the urgency required. Wholesale problems are rarely amenable to wholesale solutions, and seeking to offer mass medicines for a mass malaise is usually a form of illusion mongering. The real answer to the papers will be in lives, not books.

But having noted this caution, what can we say in the face of the papers? One thing is perfectly clear. Their main thrust is quite obvious and can be appreciated without my help, his understanding of fools or any other intermediary. It is frequently said that in time of war it is as foolish to believe everything that comes from the other side as it is not to believe anything. The same must apply here. The other side too are victims of their own premises and propaganda; and in any case, no one can claim to have modernity by the scruff of the neck. "If the shoe fits, wear it" must therefore be as applicable to the fight of faith in the modern world as anywhere else. The evidence of which the other side speaks is there for any one of us to observe and verify. We are each as free (and responsible) to draw our own conclusions as they have theirs. We must therefore begin by asking: What are they saying? Is it true? Then what of it?

Undoubtedly there is one central question which cannot be escaped by any who confess that Jesus Christ is Lord. Is the church in the Western world culturally captive, more shortsighted and more worldly than she realizes? Are we ourselves? If so, what will be the outcome?

What is historically certain is that cultural conformity is never the end of the story for the church, any more than it was for the nation of Israel. To both, God has said: When you want to become like other nations, . . . "you are thinking of something that can never be."[4] Cultural conformity, it seems, is only a stop on the line. That line either doubles back through grace to renewal and reformation or continues straight on to judgment and destruction.

Renewal and reformation, or judgment and destruction? In the modern situation this choice constitutes an awesome challenge, and the outcome must inevitably depend partly on each one of us. For the fact is that our real enemy today is not secularism, not humanism, not Marxism, not any of the great religious rivals to the Christian gospel, not even modernization, but ourselves. We who are Western Christians are simply a special case of a universal human condition to which Pascal pointed earlier. "Jesus Christ comes to tell men that they have no enemies but themselves."[5] Or as it has been put more recently: "We have met the enemy and it is us."[6]

Fortunately, perhaps, we do not know the outcome of our story. But for myself, having pondered these papers, I agree with my source that bleak pessimism must not be the end. Just as he said, as soon as we turn from the present to the future and from the central problem to its possible remedies, the fool's-eye view shows the way through.

*Facing the facts.*   First, the fool's-eye view helps us in facing the situation. It enables us to assess the facts realistically and yet to see that the apparently pessimistic picture (and naturally pessimistic response) must not be taken entirely at face value. We have seen how the European believer is likely to be unduly discouraged about the state of the faith, and the American believer overly enthusiastic, simply because of their different spiritual surroundings. In the same way, many of us who have been suddenly forced to expand our horizons and take a broad view of the Western church in the modern world may feel overwhelmed. The picture appears to close in like an unbroken panorama of pessimism.

But without minimizing the gravity of our situation, the fool's-eye view provides a double corrective, because on at least two accounts the pessimism may be rooted more in impressions than facts. To begin with, part of the discouragement may be rooted in the feelings which inevitably follow a switch from the bits-and-pieces thinking (to which many of us are accustomed) to a more comprehensive view of the whole. Like an inactive, middle-aged man who is suddenly forced to run, the bits-and-pieces thinkers are compelled to exert themselves at a level they are not used to, and they feel pain in muscles of which they were not previously aware. But like the runner's, this pain passes with exercise, leaving us ready to "think globally but act locally," a basic requirement of contemporary discipleship.

Another part of the discouragement may be rooted in the discomfort of being forced to see things from the other side's point of view. Inside-out, back-to-front thinking can be dizzying at first. But it can also train us in the mental and spiritual agility that eventually allows us to join with the subversive table turning of the fool maker and refuse to bow to the tyranny and finality of the here and now.

I would not deny that the facts of the wider situation struck me as very troubling, even painful, quite apart from any personal complicity as a modern Christian. But the fool maker's sense of discrepancy between the real and the apparent is crucial here. The current facts are not the complete facts.

Some of the bleakness of the papers is simply because theirs is a perspective on the church "under the sun." Modern ecclesiastics and ancient Ecclesiastes come around to the same conclusion: Leave out God and the high demands of his ways, and we soon find we have exchanged the "holy of holies" for "vanity of vanities." That so much of what we are doing today can be explained so adequately by categories "under the sun" must be a measure of our worldliness. "Under the sun" the church amounts to little; under the Son she can aspire to and achieve much.

In addition, for all the comprehensiveness of their sorry catalog of worldliness and failure, what is striking in the papers is the arrogance behind all they overlook. Yet it is not surprising that in a world of the big, the powerful and the well known, most of the staggering victories and the true Christian heroes are unnoticed and unsung. These Christians are the hidden resistance fighters of our generation, those whose solid character and simple lives have a worth more substantial than fame, a greatness surpassing any conferred by stardom. Topsy-turvily, they remain unsung, but they are the true just ones. Known only to God, they are those without whom no church, no community, no country can long endure.

Thus the challenge of the present facts is neither harder nor easier for us than it was for the earliest believers who had to say yes to Christ and no to Caesar. What matters finally is faith, the stance from which the discrepancy is seen, from which the facts are best assessed and from which action most effectively proceeds. God, after all, is sovereign over the wider picture and not just over our own small part.

*Playing the rebound.*    Second, the fool's-eye view helps us to assess the rivals to the Christian faith and to answer them. There is every reason to believe that the major alternatives to the gospel are in worse condition than the church. In the case of secularism, for example, the plainest fact about the secular world is its disillusionment with secularism. Heralded so recently as progressive and irreversible, secularism (the philosophy) has failed conspicuously to consolidate the advantages offered to it by secularization (the process). There are more atheistic and nonreligious people in the world than ever before, as the papers attest, but there is a ferment of new spiritual movements which grows straight from the heart of the problems with secularism.

People in the secular world have too much to live with, too little to live for. Once growth and prosperity cease to be their reason for existence, they ask questions about the purpose and meaning of their lives: Whence? Whither? Why? To such questions secularism has no answer, or—more accurately—the answers it has given have not satisfied in practice. Secularism in its sophisticated humanist form is too erudite at times, too banal at others; it flourishes only in intellectual centers. In its repressive Marxist form, it creaks.

In the long term, there is no lasting substitute for religion. Sometimes for better, usually for worse, religion is the only substitute for religion. As a modern playwright put the problem, "Without worship you shrink; it's as brutal as that."[7]

It is possible that our generation is standing on the threshold of a rebound of historic proportions. The modern world has come of age and rejected the outgrown tutelage of faith. But its prodigal descent has been swift. In the same vein as the papers, we could list our own ironies. Modern cities make people closer yet stranger at once; modern weapons bring their users to the point of impotence and destruction simultaneously; modern media promise facts but deliver fantasies; modern education introduces mass schooling but fosters sub-literacy; modern technologies of communication encourage people to speak more and say less and to hear more and listen less; modern lifestyles offer do-it-yourself freedom but slavishly follow fads; modern styles of relationships make people hungry for intimacy and authenticity but more fearful than ever of phoniness, manipulation and power games. And so on.

If this is so, we may be poised on the brink of the *reductio ad absurdum* of modern secularism. But then the question is this: How will people be turned, like the source of these papers, not only from secularism but from the post-Christian religious alternatives as well? How do we speak to an age made spiritually deaf by its skepticism and morally colorblind by its relativism? The prosaic sermon and the labored apology have proved ineffective, as stolid and single-visioned as the flat-earth literalism of the secularized mind itself. One contribution must surely come from a wide rediscovery of the prophetic fool making of the divine subversive. but only once the tables have been turned on us.

**The West is not the world.**    Third, the fool's-eye view reminds us that our talk of the modern church needs balancing, for the modern church is not all the church. Indeed, it is the smaller as well as the spiritually poorer part. Beyond it stirs the youthful energy and expanding vision of the church in the less-developed world. Less modernized, it is less worldly. Less sophisticated, it is less secular. Lagging behind in modernization, it may soon be leading in ministry, its dedication, sacrifice and joy a transfusion of life to the withered churches in Europe and the worldly wise faith in America.

After centuries as the dominant faith of Europe, Christianity has become the first truly universal faith in world history. Its color has already shifted back decisively from white to nonwhite, just as its center is now shifting from Europe to Africa and Asia.

This fact carries its own illusions. Expressed unguardedly, it creates the misleading impression that the only Christians who truly flourish are the less educated ones in the Third World or the persecuted ones in the Eastern bloc, those not exposed to the tempting power and prosperity of the modern world.

How they will fare when the blandishments of modernity come their way is another question, and one they will face in their own time. But for the moment, the greater illusion is that of the indispensability of the church in the modern world. The Western church is not the whole church. It is only the older church, a church which handed on its torch just as it was taken captive by the world it had helped to create. But what if that torch were handed back to the old church by the new, burning more brightly than when it was given? The challenge of modernity would still have to be faced, but with all the lessons of our experience and all the life of theirs.

*No fear for the Faith.* Fourth, the fool's-eye view sees that the faith will endure, because of the faith itself. Even if the modern world proved to be the greatest challenge the church has faced, or if the alternatives to the gospel were powerful and menacing rather than weak, or if the church in the rest of the world were nonexistent or as weak as we are, the faith would still endure. Its currency is truth; its source an unconquerable kingdom.

The Christian church may be in poor shape in the modern world, but this is not the first time, nor is it likely to be the last. As always, when the church is compromised by its cultural alliances, it suffers along with the culture to which it conforms. It may thus suffer doubly, once as the price of its compromise, and once as the price of its identification with a culture under judgment by God. This double judgment could be the fate of the Western church.

Yet the kingdom of God can never be totally absorbed into any cultural system. There will always be part of it which does not fit, which cannot be squeezed into any social or cultural mold. Christian truth is finally irreducible and intractable, and it is here, in the inescapable tension of its being "in" but not "of" the world, that the possibility of some future judgment or liberation lies.

Marxism, by contrast, lacks such resilience because it lacks such transcendence. As David Martin points out, "It is a paradox that a system which claimed that the beginning of all criticism was the criticism of religion should have ended up with a form of religion which was the end of criticism."[8] *Pravda* in Russian means "truth," but truth in Russia has been mastered by *Pravda*.

What is the secret of Christianity's capacity to survive repeated periods of cultural captivity? On the one hand, it has in God's Word an authority that stands higher than history, a judgment that is ultimately irreducible to any generation and culture. On the other hand, it has in its notion of sin and repentance a doctrine of its own failure which can be the wellspring of its ongoing criticism and renewal.

Like an eternal jack-in-the-box, Christian truth will always spring back. No power on earth can finally keep it down, not even the power of Babylonian confusion and captivity. "At least five times," noted G. K. Chesterton, "the Faith has to all appearances gone to the dogs. In each of these five cases, it was the dog that died."[9]

To write these things is not to whistle in the dark. Nor to dredge up arguments to bolster the defenses of a sagging optimism. Rather, since the Gravedigger thesis turns on the monumental irony with which the papers began, it is apt to finish with another: There is no one like the other side for overplaying their hand.

Out of corruption came Reformation. This was the story of their sixteenth-century overbalance. But what of an earlier day still, a day when they planned another grave and held another body captive?

That day witnessed the greatest irony of all. It was, as John Donne said, the day death died.[10] Because, as Augustine had said before him, the cross of the Lord was "the devil's mousetrap."[11]

Grave digging has been a somewhat less than certain business ever since.

# Notes

## Memo 1: Operation Gravedigger

[1]See Peter L. Berger, *The Social Reality of Religion* (Harmondsworth, Eng.: Penguin, 1973), p. 132; published in the United States as *The Sacred Canopy* (Garden City, N.Y.: Doubleday, Anchor Books, 1969); see also David Martin, *The Dilemmas of Contemporary Religion* (Oxford: Blackwell, 1978), p. 54; Roland Robertson, *The Sociological Interpretation of Religion* (Oxford: Blackwell, 1970), p. 43.

[2]Noel Annan, *Leslie Stephen* (London: MacGibbon and Kee, 1951), p. 110.

[3]Quoted in Ian Bradley, *The Call to Seriousness* (London: Jonathan Cape, 1976), p. 15.

[4]Quoted in Paul W. Blackstock, *The Strategy of Subversion* (Chicago: Quadrangle Books, 1964), p. 51.

[5]See Noel Barber, *Sinister Twilight* (London: Fontana Collins, 1970).

[6]Romans 1:25.

[7]"Letters on a Regicide Peace," letter 1, in *The Work of Edmund Burke*, vol. 6 (London: Oxford Univ. Press, 1907), p. 85.

[8]H. Richard Niebuhr, *Christ and Culture* (New York: Harper, Colophon Books, 1975), p. xi.
[9]Peter L. Berger and Richard Neuhaus, eds., *Against the World for the World* (New York: Seabury Press, 1976).
[10]See 1 Samuel 4:1-11; 2 Samuel 6:1-9; Jeremiah 7:1-15; Mark 3:1-6; Romans 1—7; Jeremiah 1:10.

**Memo 2: The Sandman Effect**
[1]See Bernard Crick, *George Orwell: A Life* (Harmondsworth, Eng.: Penguin, 1982), p. 500.
[2]Quoted in Herbert R. Lottman, *The Left Bank* (Boston: Houghton Mifflin, 1982), p. 23.
[3]See Peter L. Berger and Thomas Luckmann, *The Social Construction of Reality* (Harmondsworth, Eng.: Penguin, 1967), pp. 174ff.; Berger, *The Social Reality of Religion*, chap. 2.
[4]1 Timothy 3:15 (NEB).
[5]See Sidney A. Burrell, ed., *The Role of Religion in Modern European History* (New York: Macmillan, 1964), p. 95.
[6]See Owen Chadwick, *The Secularization of the European Mind in the Nineteenth Century* (Cambridge: Cambridge Univ. Press, 1975), pp. 1-18.
[7]See Berger, *Social Construction of Reality*, pp. 1-30.
[8]Blaise Pascal, *Pensées* (3. 60), trans. A. J. Krailsheimer (Harmondsworth, Eng.: Penguin, 1966), p. 46.
[9]In the Louvre Museum, Paris.
[10]See Robin Gill, *Social Context of Theology* (Oxford: Mowbrays, 1975), chap. 4.
[11]Jacques Ellul, *The New Demons* (Oxford: Mowbrays, 1975), p. 19.

**Memo 3: The Cheshire-Cat Factor**
[1]Quoted in Alistair Cooke, *Six Men* (Harmondsworth, Eng.: Penguin, 1978), p. 13.
[2]*Prospects for the Eighties* (London: Bible Society, 1980), p. 12.
[3]*The Times Literary Supplement*, 18 Dec. 1981, p. 1461.
[4]Ellul, *New Demons*, p. 2.
[5]See Berger, *Social Reality of Religion*, pp. 113ff.; David Martin, *A General Theory of Secularization* (Oxford: Blackwell, 1978); Martin E. Marty, *The Modern Schism* (London: SCM, 1969); Bryan R. Wilson, *Religion in Secular Society* (London: C. A. Watts, 1966).
[6]David Barrett, ed., *World Christian Encyclopedia* (Oxford: Oxford Univ. Press, 1982).
[7]Ibid.
[8]Chadwick, *Secularization of European Mind*, p. 9.
[9]Quoted in ibid., p. 18.
[10]See Berger and Neuhaus, *Against the World*, chap. 1.
[11]Ibid., p. 10.
[12]Barrett, *World Christian Encyclopedia*.
[13]Ibid.
[14]*Christianity Today*, 19 Feb. 1982, p. 28.

[15]See Chadwick, *Secularization of European Mind*, p. 97.
[16]See Joseph N. Moody, "The Dechristianization of the French Working Class," in Burrell, *Role of Religion*, pp. 89ff.
[17]Quoted in *Context*, 15 Nov. 1981, p. 6 (emphasis added).
[18]See Martin, *General Theory of Secularization*, p. 3.
[19]See Peter L. Berger, "From Secularity to World Religions," *The Christian Century*, 16 Jan. 1980, pp. 41-45.
[20]See Berger, *Social Reality of Religion*, p. 114.
[21]See Martin, *General Theory of Secularization*, p. 84.
[22]See Marty, *Modern Schism*, chap. 4; Michael Argyle and Benjamin Beit-Hallahmi, *The Social Psychology of Religion* (London: Routledge and Kegan Paul, 1975), pp. 25-29.
[23]See Moody, "Dechristianization," in Burrell, *Role of Religion*, p. 90.

**Memo 4: The Private-Zoo Factor**
[1]See Peter L. Berger, Brigitte Berger and Hansfried Kellner, *The Homeless Mind* (Harmondsworth, Eng.: Penguin, 1974), chap. 3.
[2]See Peter L. Berger, *Facing Up to Modernity* (New York: Basic Books, 1977), chap. 11; Arthur Brittan, *The Privatised World* (London: Routledge and Kegan Paul, 1978)
[3]See Thorstein Veblen, *The Theory of the Leisure Class* (New York: New American Library, 1953).
[4]Berger, *Facing Modernity*, p. 18.
[5]Theodore Roszak, *Where the Wasteland Ends* (New York: Doubleday, 1973), p. 449.
[6]Peter Brown, *Augustine of Hippo* (London: Faber and Faber, 1967), p. 248.
[7]Karl Mannheim, *Essays on the Sociology of Knowledge* (London: Routledge and Kegan Paul, 1952), p. 269.
[8]See Berger et al., *Homeless Mind*, pp. 167ff.
[9]See ibid., p. 168; also Christopher Lasch, *The Culture of Narcissism* (New York: W. W. Norton, 1979).
[10]*Christianity Today*, 12 Nov. 1982, p. 80.
[11]Bryan R. Wilson, *Contemporary Transformations of Religion* (Oxford: Oxford Univ. Press, 1976), p. 87.
[12]See C. W. Mills, *The Sociological Imagination* (Harmondsworth, Eng.: Penguin, 1970), pp. 188, 189; cf. Berger et al., *Homeless Mind*, p. 168.
[13]George Orwell, *Decline of the English Murder and other Essays* (Harmondsworth, Eng.: Penguin, 1965), p. 79.
[14]See Alexander Solzhenitsyn et al., *From under the Rubble* (New York: Bantam, 1976); Martin, *Dilemmas of Contemporary Religion*, pp. 75ff.

**Memo 5: The Smorgasbord Factor**
[1]See Berger, *Social Reality of Religion*, pp. 138ff.
[2]See ibid., chap. 2.
[3]Martin, *Dilemmas of Contemporary Religion*, p. 168.
[4]See ibid., pp. 1ff.
[5]See Barrett, *World Christian Encyclopedia*.

[6]See Berger and Luckmann, *Social Construction of Reality*, pp. 102ff.; Berger et al., *Homeless Mind*, pp. 64-65.

[7]Quoted in *The Observer*, 19 Apr. 1981, p. 13.

[8]Quoted in Peter Williamson and Kevin Perrotta, eds., *Christianity Confronts Modernity* (Ann Arbor, Mich.: Servant Books, 1981), p. 12.

[9]Ibid.

[10]Quoted in *Context*, 15 Dec. 1981, p. 6.

[11]See Peter L. Berger, *The Heretical Imperative* (Garden City, N.Y.: Doubleday, 1979), chap. 1.

[12]See Peter L. Berger, *The Precarious Vision* (Garden City, N.Y.: Doubleday, 1961), pp. 17ff.

[13]Lasch, *Culture of Narcissism*, p. 14.

[14]See Wilson, *Religion in Secular Society*, pp. 51-52.

[15]Quoted in Gill, *Social Context of Theology*, p. 100.

[16]Quoted in *The Times Literary Supplement*, 28 Jan. 1983, p. 83.

**Memo 6: European-Style Confusion**

[1]"Ballad of a Thin Man," *Highway 61 Revisited*.

[2]Quoted in Paul W. Blackstock, *Agents of Deceit* (Chicago: Quadrangle Books, 1966), p. 38.

[3]Joseph Kraft, quoted in Franky Schaeffer, *A Time for Anger* (Westchester, Ill.: Crossway, 1982), p. 192.

[4]*Areopagitica* (London: J. M. Dent, 1927), p. 32.

[5]*The Note-Books of Samuel Butler* (London: Jonathan Cape, 1926), p. 263.

[6]Edward Ross, quoted in Paul W. Blackstock, *Agents of Deceit*, p. 17.

[7]Quoted in ibid., p. 18.

[8]*Erewhon Revisited* (London: J. M. Dent, 1932), p. 293.

[9]See Keith Thomas, *Religion and the Decline of Magic* (London: Weidenfeld and Nicolson, 1971), p. 173.

[10]See Peter L. Berger, *A Rumor of Angels* (Garden City, N.Y.: Doubleday, 1970), chap. 2.

[11]See Martin, *General Theory of Secularization*, pp. 272ff.

[12]Quoted in Roland H. Bainton, *Erasmus of Christendom* (New York: Scribners, 1969), p. 58.

[13]Quoted in ibid., p. 117.

[14]See Wallace K. Ferguson, "The Church in a Changing World," in Burrell, *Role of Religion*.

[15]See Chadwick, *Secularization of European Mind*, p. 213.

[16]Quoted in ibid., p. 156.

[17]Quoted in ibid., p. 216.

[18]Quoted in ibid., p. 156.

[19]See David Martin, *The Religious and the Secular* (London: Routledge and Kegan Paul, 1969), pp. 9ff.; Chadwick, *Secularization of European Mind*, pp. 264ff.

**Memo 7: American-Style Counterfeits**

[1]See Robert N. Bellah, "Civil Religion in America," *Daedalus* 96, no. 1 (Winter 1967);

Robert D. Linder and Richard V. Pierard, *Twilight of the Saints* (Downers Grove, Ill.: InterVarsity Press, 1978).
[2]See Michael J. Malbin, *Religion and Politics* (Washington, D.C.: American Enterprise Institute, 1978).
[3]See Berger, *Social Reality of Religion*, chap. 6.
[4]Quoted in Marty, *Modern Schism*, p. 139.
[5]Quoted in James S. Tinney, "The Prosperity Doctrine," *Spirit*, Apr. 1978.
[6]Quoted in Frank S. Mead, *Handbook of Denominations* (Nashville: Abingdon, 1970), p. 217.
[7]Quoted in *Context*, 15 Feb. 1982, p. 6.
[8]See Raymond Williams, *Communications* (Harmondsworth, Eng.: Penguin, 1970).
[9]David Rosenthal, "Kid Power?" *Bostonia*, Winter 1979, p. 13.
[10]Quoted in Cynthia Schaible, "The Gospel of the Good Life," *Eternity*, Feb. 1981, p. 21.
[11]Jack Newfield, *A Prophetic Minority* (New York: Signet Books, 1967), p. 157.
[12]Horace Bushnell, quoted in Marty, *Modern Schism*, p. 132.
[13]Quoted in Schaible, "Gospel of Good Life," p. 22.
[14]Quoted in Martin, *Dilemmas of Contemporary Religion*, p. viii.
[15]Quoted in P. Fitzgerald, *The Knox Brothers* (London: Macmillan, 1979), p. 259.

**Memo 8: Damage to Enemy Institutions**
[1]See Jürgen Habermas, *Legitimation Crisis* (Boston: Beacon Press, 1973), p. 90.
[2]Andrew M. Greeley, *The Persistence of Religion* (London: SCM, 1973), p. 14.
[3]See Berger, *Social Reality of Religion*, p. 133.
[4]Martin, *General Theory of Secularization*, p. 71.
[5]See Martin, *Dilemmas of Contemporary Religion*, p. 53.
[6]Peter L. Berger, "The Second Children's Crusade," *The Christian Century*, 2 Dec. 1959.
[7]Lasch, *Culture of Narcissism*.
[8]Daniel J. Boorstin, *The Image* (New York: Atheneum, 1962), p. 57.
[9]Luke 6:26 (NIV).
[10]See Berger, *Social Reality of Religion*, pp. 143-48.
[11]See Ivan Illich, *Disabling Professions* (London: Marion Boyars, 1977).

**Memo 9: Damage to Enemy Ideas**
[1]Quoted in *Time*, 7 June 1976, p. 54.
[2]Quoted in Schaible, "Gospel of Good Life," p. 26.
[3]Exodus 10:26 (NEB).
[4]See Boorstin, *Image*, pp. 130ff.
[5]Quoted in *Sojourners*, Jan. 1978, p. 9.
[6]G. K. Chesterton, "What I Saw in America," in Raymond T. Bond, ed., *The Man Who Was Chesterton* (New York: Dodd Mead, 1946), p. 235.
[7]Quoted in Linder and Pierard, *Twilight of Saints*, p. 164.

**Memo 10: Fossils and Fanatics**
[1]See Berger, *Facing Modernity*, pp. 175ff.; Berger, *Social Reality of Religion*, pp. 157ff.

[2]See Martin, *Dilemmas of Contemporary Religion*, pp. 75ff.
[3]See Berger, *Rumor of Angels*, pp. 17, 18.
[4]See ibid., pp. 13, 14.
[5]See Martin, *General Theory of Secularization*, pp. 111ff.
[6]See Peter L. Berger, *Invitation to Sociology* (Harmondsworth, Eng.: Penguin, 1966), pp. 130, 131.
[7]Quoted in Chadwick, *Secularization of European Mind*, p. 250.
[8]Burrell, *Role of Religion*, p. 94.

**Memo 11: Trendies and Traitors**

[1]See Berger, *Facing Modernity*, pp. 169ff.
[2]Ibid.
[3]See Henry Chadwick, "All Things to All Men," *New Testament Studies*, 1954-55, pp. 261-75.
[4]See Berger, *Facing Modernity*, p. 165.
[5]Ibid., p. 168.
[6]See Antoine Lion, in David Martin, John Orme Mills and W. S. F. Pickering, eds., *Sociology and Theology: Alliance and Conflict* (Brighton, Eng.: Harvester Press, 1980), pp. 163-82.
[7]George Tyrell, *Christianity at the Cross-roads* (London: Allen and Unwin, 1963), p. 49.
[8]Albert Schweitzer, *The Quest for the Historical Jesus* (London: A. & C. Black, 1954), p. 398.
[9]See Berger, *Rumor of Angels*, p. 41.
[10]Ibid., p. 23.
[11]Walter Kaufmann, *The Faith of a Heretic* (New York: New American Library, 1959), p. 32.
[12]Berger, *Rumor of Angels*, pp. 20, 21.
[13]Alasdair Macintyre and Paul Ricoeur, *The Religious Significance of Atheism* (New York: Columbia Univ. Press, 1969), p. 46.
[14]Walter Kaufmann, *Existentialism, Religion and Death* (New York: New American Library, 1976), p. 3.
[15]Macintyre and Ricoeur, *Religious Significance of Atheism*, p. 29.
[16]See Ellul, *New Demons*, p. 38.
[17]Berger, *Rumor of Angels*, p. 12.
[18]Berger, *Facing Modernity*, p. 163.

**Afterword**

[1]Czeslaw Milosz, *Visions from San Francisco Bay* (Manchester, Eng.: Carcanet New Press, 1982), p. 74.
[2]Malcolm Muggeridge, *Christ and the Media* (London: Hodder and Stoughton, 1977), p. 76.
[3]Reinhold Schneider, *Imperial Mission*, trans. Walter Oden (New York: Gresham Press, 1948), p. 93.
[4]Ezekiel 20:32 (NEB).

⁵*Pensées* (4. 433), trans. Krailsheimer, p. 164.

⁶Walt Kelly, *Pogo* comic strip.

⁷Peter Shaffer, *Equus,* Act 2, in *Three Plays* (Harmondsworth, Eng.: Penguin, 1976), p. 274.

⁸D. Martin, *Dilemmas of Contemporary Religion,* p. 88.

⁹*The Everlasting Man* (Garden City, N.Y.: Doubleday, Image Books, 1955), pp. 260, 261.

¹⁰"Holy Sonnet X," in *Donne: Poetical Works* (Oxford: Oxford Univ. Press, 1971), p. 297.

¹¹*Sermo* 130. 2.